Before the Wave:
Puerto Ricans in Philadelphia,
1910–1945

Before the Wave:
Puerto Ricans in Philadelphia, 1910–1945

Víctor Vázquez-Hernández

Printed in the United States of America

Library of Congress Cataloging—in-Publication Data
Names: Vázquez-Hernández, Víctor, 1952- author.
Title: Before the wave : Puerto Ricans in Philadelphia, 1910-1945 / Víctor Vázquez-Hernández.
Description: New York, NY : Centro Press, Center for Puerto Rican Studies, Hunter College, CUNY, [2016] | Includes bibliographical references and index.
Identifiers: LCCN 2016047262 (print) | LCCN 2017002220 (ebook) | ISBN 9781945662027 (paperback : acid-free paper) | ISBN 9781945662034 (ebook)
Subjects: LCSH: Puerto Ricans--Pennslvania--Philadelphia--History--20th century. | Puerto Ricans--Pennslvania--Philadelphia--Social conditions--20th century. | Community life--Pennslvania--Philadelphia--History--20th century. | Immigrants--Pennslvania--Philadelphia--History--20th century. | Philadelphia (Pa.)--Ethnic relations--History--20th century. | Philadelphia (Pa.)--Emigration and immigration--History--20th century. | Puerto Rico--Emigration and immigration--History--20th century.
Classification: LCC F158.9.P85 V38 2016 (print) | LCC F158.9.P85 (ebook) | DDC 305.868/729507481150904--dc23
LC record available at https://lccn.loc.gov/2016047262

Centro Press
Center for Puerto Rican Studies
Hunter College, CUNY
695 Park Avenue, E-1429
New York, NY 10065
centrops@hunter.cuny.edu
http://centropr.hunter.cuny.edu

Dedicated to my wife, Mayra Lee Hernandez-Ruiz,
who for the past 23 years has supported and cheered me on
to complete this project. Her love and skill in the study
of Genealogy has been a great inspiration!
Gracias!

TABLE OF CONTENTS

LIST OF ILLUSTRATIONS

PROLOGUE
By Carmen Teresa Whalen

In *Before the Wave: Puerto Ricans in Philadelphia, 1910-1945*, Víctor Vázquez-Hernández tells a story that is important in its own right, as well as one that makes important contributions to other stories already told and yet to be told. This is the first book on Puerto Ricans in Philadelphia in the interwar years. Here, we learn that Puerto Ricans, who came to the city, were cigar makers and political exiles, seeking to overthrow Spain's colonial rule in Puerto Rico and Cuba. They were also students, merchants, and professionals. Settling in several distinct neighborhoods, Puerto Ricans joined and added to the city's racial and ethnic diversity. Through their social, cultural, and religious activities, they built Puerto Rican communities and were part of a diverse and vibrant pan-Latina/o community. An important and overlooked dimension of Philadelphia's interwar period, these early Puerto Rican migrants also laid the foundations for the dramatic increase in Puerto Rican migration after World War II. In telling this compelling story of Puerto Rican Philadelphia between the World Wars, Vázquez-Hernández uncovers a buried history and makes important contributions in several areas.

With *Before the Wave*, Philadelphia takes its proper place in the histories of the early Puerto Rican diaspora. Previous scholarship has focused on the Puerto Rican community in New York City. This work began with Virginia Sánchez Korrol's foundational community study, *From Colonia to Community: The History of Puerto Ricans in New York City*, first published in 1983, and then Ruth Glasser's *My Music is My Flag: Puerto Rican Musicians and Their New York Communities 1917-1940*, published over a decade later in 1995. More recently, Lorrin Thomas's *Puerto Rican Citizen: History and Political Identity in Twentieth Century New York City* includes chapters on the interwar period within a broader chronological scope. Although the Puerto Rican community in the interwar era was largest in New York City, Puerto Ricans settled elsewhere, and the scholarship has started to reflect that. Scholars have explored Puerto Ricans' early migration to Hawai'i, where they were recruited as contracted laborers to work on sugar plantations beginning in 1900 (see López 2005; López and Forbes 2001). Puerto Ricans also migrated in significant numbers to Florida and California. Yet most of the scholarship on the interwar period has focused on the larger Latina/o groups in these areas—Cubans in Florida and Mexican-Americans in California.

With Vázquez-Hernández's contribution, we can now begin to think more comparatively about what we know about the early Puerto Rican diaspora. *Before the Wave* highlights the importance of the racial and ethnic composition of the places where Puerto Ricans settled, while providing a more nuanced portrayal of Philadelphia's racial and ethnic diversity. This pioneering generation lived and worked among Spaniards, Mexicans, and Cubans, as well as other national origin groups. Beyond this Spanish-speaking community, Vázquez-Hernández considers the city's white ethnic and African American communities. Puerto Ricans' working lives, neighborhoods, and community building took shape within that diversity, as Vázquez-Hernández so vibrantly depicts. He is among a growing number of scholars contributing to new research that moves beyond an exclusive portrait of a single national origin group, which has characterized immigration, ethnic, American, and Latina/o Studies. *Before the Wave* uncovers and acknowledges the greater complexities of inter-racial and inter-ethnic relations that shaped people's lives (Rúa 2012).

In addition, Vázquez-Hernández closely examines how political and economic ties shaped the migration to Philadelphia, as well as the types of jobs available to Puerto Ricans who settled in the city. Here, he draws on foundational works of the Centro de Estudios Puertorriqueños, History Task Force's 1979 *Labor Migration Under Capitalism: The Puerto Rican Experience*, and contributes to more recent scholarship that places migration firmly within the context of both the colonial relationship between Puerto Rico and the United States, and the global economy (Whalen 2001; Pérez 2004; Fernández 2012). As a result, his approach provides a more nuanced look at the vibrant working-class community that emerged. At the same time, he sheds light on the socioeconomic diversity within this early Puerto Rican community by highlighting the students, merchants, and professionals, who also comprised the interwar community, sometimes assuming leadership roles. Through his use of a wide range of historical sources, Vázquez-Hernández depicts another level of migration too often missed—the workings of networks of individuals, the functioning of interpersonal relationships, the stories of real people.

This important foundational work on Puerto Ricans in Philadelphia between the World Wars also provides a critical link to the Great Migration of the post-World War II era. Indeed, most of the scholarship on Puerto Rican migration has focused on the period from the post-World War II era to the present, without the benefit of a firm foundation in the earlier period. I can only ponder the ways in which my own work on Puerto Rican migration to Philadelphia in the postwar era would have been enriched had I been able to build upon this earlier period, with Vázquez-Hernández 's scholarship establishing such a rich foundation (Whalen 2001). In Philadelphia, this early community set the contours for social networks, and for residential settlement and employment patterns, as well as for community and institution building. Ultimately, Vázquez-Hernández reminds us that Latina/o diversity is not just a post-1965 Immigration Reform Act phenomenon. Rather, Puerto Ricans, as well as other Latinas/os, have deep historical roots and a long and rich history in the United States.

REFERENCES

Centro de Estudios Puertorriqueños, History Task Force. 1979. *Labor Migration Under Capitalism: The Puerto Rican Experience*. New York: Monthly Review Press.

Fernández, Lilia. 2012. *Brown in the Windy City: Mexicans and Puerto Ricans in Postwar Chicago*. Chicago: University of Chicago Press.

Glasser, Ruth. 1995. *My Music is My Flag: Puerto Rican Musicians and Their New York Communities 1917-1940*. Berkeley: University of California Press.

López, Iris. 2005. Borinkis and Chop Suey: Puerto Rican Identity Hawai'i. In *The Puerto Rican Diaspora: Historical Perspectives,* eds. Carmen Teresa Whalen and Víctor Vásquez-Hernández. 43–67. Philadelphia: Temple University Press.

López, Iris and David Forbes. 2001. Borinki Identity in Hawai'i: Present and Future. *CENTRO: Journal of the Center for Puerto Rican Studies* 13(1): 82–93.

Pérez, Gina M. 2004. *The Near Northwest Side Story: Migration Displacement and Puerto Rican Families*. Berkeley: University of California Press.

Rúa, Mérida M. 2012. *A Grounded Identidad: Making New Lives in Chicago's Puerto Rican Neighborhoods*. New York: Oxford University Press.

Sánchez Korrol, Virginia. 1994 [1983]. *From Colonia to Community: The History of Puerto Ricans in New York City*. Berkeley: University of California Press.

Thomas, Lorrin. 2010. *Puerto Rican Citizen: History and Political Identity in Twentieth Century New York City*. Chicago: University of Chicago Press.\

Whalen, Carmen Teresa. 2001. *From Puerto Rico to Philadelphia: Puerto Rican Workers and Postwar Economies*. Philadelphia, Temple University Press.

ACKNOWLEDGEMENTS

As often happens with endeavors like this book, while rewarding it has been made possible by the support and collaboration of many individuals. I have the deepest appreciation of three individuals whose family's stories bring life to this manuscript. Jesse Bermudez-Malpica, founder of the *Asociacion de Musicos Latino Americanos* (AMLA), Philadelphia's Latino musicians Union was incredibly generous and kind with his time as he introduced me to the life of his cigar maker father, Antonio Malpica. Maria Pajil, who introduced me to her 90-year-old grandmother, Mary Rodriguez afforded me the opportunity to sense what it was like to live in 1930s Philadelphia and Zoraida Figueroa opened her house to me so I could speak with her father Juan Canales. Even after the passing of Mary Rodriguez and Juan Canales, I was able to go back and speak with Mary's daughter, Emma who was born in Philadelphia in the 1930s and acquire additional information about her mother and get pictures as well. I am truly indebted to all of them. I also want to thank Rosa Santiago and Cynthia Alvarez for their respective insight and personal knowledge of the Puerto Ricans who lived in Southwark and progressively moved to South Philadelphia, through them I learned about this important enclave.

The archival research conducted at La Milagrosa Church was instrumental in understanding the experience of early Puerto Ricans and the other Latinos in Philadelphia through the rich information gleaned from wedding and baptismal records. Thank you to all the staff there. In the different archives I visited I found tremendously helpful and dedicated staff. Margaret Jerrido and her staff at the Temple University Urban Archives, where I conducted the bulk of my archival research were fantastic and very patient and supportive. The same holds true for the staff at the Centro de Estudios Puertorriqueños Archives at Hunter College especially Pedro Juan Hernandez as well as the Archivo General in San Juan, Puerto Rico. I appreciate the work and assistance of Dr. Edwin Aponte for his many writings on the work of the First Spanish Baptist Church in Philadelphia and for early comments on my work.

Originally a doctoral dissertation project, this manuscript benefitted incredibly by the able and critical guidance of the Dr. Kenneth L. Kusmer, historian extraordinaire at Temple University, as well the patient and skillful feedback from Dr. Arthur Schmidt and Dr. James Hilty. There were many, too many to single out doctoral students with whom I took several seminars who commented on early version of the chapters. I owe a great gratitude to Dr. Paul George, Dr. Manuel Rodriguez-Vazquez and Prof. Ariel Arnau, who read the complete manuscript and provided insightful critiques and asked very pertinent questions, which improved the story. I also had the opportunity to present portions of this work in numerous conferences and the feedback from my colleagues and participants was very helpful. In particular, Dr. Lorrin Thomas was one those with whom I participated in panels and critiqued the work as well as encouraged me throughout. Thank you to Dr. Aldo Lauria Santiago for providing spaces to discuss on going work on the diaspora.

I am also grateful to Dr. Edwin Melendez, Executive Director of the Centro for suggesting I submit the manuscript to them for consideration. I appreciated the timely and thoughtful guidance of the Centro's editor, Xavier Totti and for skillfully helping to bring the work to fruition. I am immensely proud to have the Center for Puerto Ricans Studies publish the book. I have been inspired throughout this work by Dr. Virginia Sanchez Korrol, pioneer in the history of the Puerto Rican diaspora in the U.S. Thank you for your path breaking and inspirational work.

Finally, I am indebted beyond words and grateful for her presence in my academic life, I offer a very special thank you to Dr. Carmen Teresa Whalen. For the past twenty years she has been a friend, a colleague, a critic and most important a visionary whom I have been humbled enough to follow. Thank you for everything you have done to make me a serious and sensitive thinker and writer of history.

CHAPTER 1

From Colonial Periphery to the Core: An Introduction

On a rainy Sunday afternoon in February, 1999, in the Frankford section of Philadelphia, Jesse (Jesus) Malpica-Bermudez reminisced about his father, Antonio Malpica. Malpica, a life-long cigar maker, had come from Puerto Rico to Philadelphia, then a mecca of the cigar industry, in 1913. For the next four decades, until his death in 1952, Malpica, along with many other Puerto Ricans saw the City as a place of opportunity. Bermudez recalled that his father owned and operated his very own cigar making shop (*chinchal*); a store front located at 803 Callowhill Street near the foot of the Benjamin Franklin Bridge in the Northern Liberties section of the City, and, had begun to teach young Jesse, his trade (Bermudez 1999). Those years when Antonio Malpica arrived in Philadelphia were significant in the settlement and expansion of the Puerto Rican presence in the city. Beginning with the granting of U.S. citizenship to Puerto Ricans in 1917, the U.S. entry into the War in Europe the same year and the end of WW II (1945), the study of this interwar period is important for understanding how such a large diaspora that exist in the twenty-first century, happened. The study of this period is also significant in understanding how a Puerto Rican community in Philadelphia evolved. Up to now, there has been no comprehensive examination of this early history. Besides the books written about Puerto Ricans in New York, very little historiographic work has been done outside of New York that makes the connection between the interwar period and the post-WW II migration.

In addition, in 2010 the U. S. Census confirmed what some scholars had been projecting for some time: there were more Puerto Ricans living in the U.S. than on the Island. In 2000, the number of Puerto Ricans living on the Island was 3,808,610 while in the U.S. the number had increased to 3,406,178. At the time projections indicated that if the trends continued during the following decade the number of Puerto Ricans stateside would surpass those on the Island. This is in fact what happened: in 2010, the population of the Island had decreased to 3,725,789 while Puerto Ricans residing in the States rose to 4,623,716 (U.S. Department of Commerce 2010). The diaspora was larger than the islanders. The significance of this phenomenon in the development one of the largest migrant populations in the U. S.

is explored in this work by studying one of its largest and oldest components: those who settled in Philadelphia.

While Puerto Ricans and their predecessors are U.S. citizens, most are considered by many Americans as foreigners. Writing about the Puerto Rican diaspora helps shed light on what in this century appears to be a shifting ethos of what it means to be an American. The scope of this study is not meant to be monumental in American ethnic history but a contribution to the ongoing debate about Puerto Ricans and other Latinos in the U.S. and their respective proper place in U.S. History.

Puerto Ricans in the United States represent the second largest Spanish-speaking group in the country, constituting more than four million inhabitants on the mainland and another almost four million on the Island. An exploration of how and why Puerto Ricans came to the U.S., however, is a question which has received limited attention from American scholars. As the United States commemorated the one hundredth anniversary of the victory of its military forces over the Spaniards (1898), its acquisition of Puerto Rico, a consequence of that war, has received scant consideration in U.S. historiography. The Puerto Rican presence in Philadelphia, the third largest concentration in a U.S. city today, has received even less attention from scholars. There have been a few studies of Puerto Ricans in Philadelphia, but all of them deal with the post-1945 period. No one has yet explored the early history of Puerto Ricans in Philadelphia. This book rectifies this scholarly deficiency by providing the first comprehensive study of Puerto Ricans in this City during the pre-World War II era.[1]

The question then becomes, why study the Puerto Rican diaspora in Philadelphia in the early part of the twentieth century? Puerto Ricans are the largest migrant group to come directly from a U.S. colonial territory. Although spread out throughout the fifty states, Puerto Ricans are still concentrated in Northeastern and Mid-western urban centers. The continued concentration in cities like New York, Chicago and Philadelphia, as well as the newer growth into the Sunbelt (Orlando and Miami) and the Southwest (Houston) among others, implies that Puerto Ricans are a significant presence in the immediate American ethnic composition of the twenty-first century as Latinos have become, numerically, the dominant minority group in the nation (Meléndez and Vargas-Ramos 2014).

Who were these Puerto Ricans that chose to migrate to Philadelphia in the early twentieth century and why they selected this particular city contributes toward illuminating our understanding of migration to Philadelphia, especially after the curtailment of European immigration in the 1920's. An exploration of the connection between these pioneer migrants and those Puerto Ricans who followed in the waves of the post-World War II "Great Migration" from the island is also important because it provides us with forward and backward linkages to this particular group, a connection that has not, until now, been explored. Some of the questions explored here ask, for instance, did the early Pan-Hispanic[2] settlements that evolved in this period in Philadelphia have any influence on where Puerto Rican migrants came to live and work? What impact did these early settlement patterns have on where the post-WW II Puerto Rican migrants settled in the city?

This is a study of the origins of the Puerto Rican community in Philadelphia with a special emphasis on the interwar years. This study connects the origins of this community to the mass migration of the post-World War II years when Puerto Ricans consolidated their presence in Philadelphia (1945–1985). This study also provides some insight into the historical development of the Puerto Rican community from the end of the twentieth into the first decades of the twenty-first centuries. To get further insight into Puerto Rican community formation, this study compares the experiences of Puerto Ricans and other Spanish-speaking immigrants during the interwar years in Philadelphia with that of the Italians, the Polish and African Americans, the premier immigrant/racial groups that also arrived in large numbers in the City in the early twentieth century.[3]

This study also argues that the picture presented by scholars on the extent and impact of Puerto Rican migration to the U.S. is seriously limited, and hampered by a lack of understanding of the pre-World War II period. In cities like New York, Philadelphia, San Francisco, Honolulu and Tampa, pre-World War II Puerto Rican migrants played a pivotal role in the post-World War II experiences of those communities, as will be demonstrated by a review of the available literature for this time period and the development of communities that have lasted well into the twenty-first century. In addition, this study further argues how important that early organizational migration experience was in carving out a significant space in which the post-World War II migration landed. These early pioneers set the tone for negotiating this community space with the larger, often hostile, non-Hispanic community of cities like Philadelphia. The bulk of available literature on Puerto Ricans in the U.S. misses this point entirely.

This book, then, helps to fill the gap in that historiography. It draws on the work of the Center for Puerto Ricans Studies on labor migration as well as the work of other scholars like Virginia Sanchez Korrol, Ruth Glasser and Lorrin Thomas as well as their respective use of historical resources and methodology; building on the community studies written by them. This book is a complimentary addition to the study of postwar Puerto Ricans in Philadelphia conducted by Carmen T. Whalen (2001). This study also builds on the pre-World War II Puerto Rican migration experience and the connections between pre- and post-war communities. It is a study beyond New York City and this comparison is important because Puerto Ricans in the U.S. have expanded and fanned out across the U.S. The historical sources and methodologies utilized in this book, most used for the first time, to study the Puerto Rican experience in Philadelphia are a contribution to further studies in this area (Sánchez-Korrol 1994).

Impact of Migration on Puerto Rican Settlement Patterns and Community Building in the U.S. — the Interwar Years

Puerto Rico's colonial status has historically shaped migration from the Island. In the later nineteenth century, Puerto Rican laborers were shipped off to the Caribbean and Central America by the Spanish colonial regime. After the U.S. took control of the Island in 1898, commercial ties between U.S. cities like Philadelphia, New York and Boston brought merchants and cigar makers to the centers of tobacco production. This connected the causes of migration with the development of the Puerto Rican diaspora in the City of Brotherly Love (Whalen 2001: 3).

Ships carrying sugar from Puerto Rico arrived regularly in Philadelphia, often-times bringing merchants who settled in the city. As the city also expanded into a major sugar processing center, more ships came and brought even larger numbers of cigar makers and other laborers. While merchants from the Island tended to settle in a variety of neighborhoods, predominantly in West Philadelphia where the more affluent Philadelphians lived, laborers and political exiles tended to settle in neighborhoods closer to the cigar industry or other industrial factories (Whalen 2001: 4).

After 1898, as a consequence of the end of the Spanish-Cuban-American war, a U.S. military government replaced the local Puerto Rican government established under Autonomist Charter granted to Puerto Ricans by Spain in 1897. For the next two years (1898–1900) the U.S. occupation dramatically altered Puerto Rico's economy and political structure. The United States effectively incorporated Puerto Rico into its sphere of influence while at the same time promoted investments in the Island as a safe bet guaranteed by American control of the island. In addition, American policy makers viewed Puerto Ricans as incapable of self-government thereby "justifying" their political imposition (Whalen 2001: 6).

A further impact of the initial U.S. occupation was the economic problems brought on by the devaluation of Puerto Rican currency, taking over lands by U.S. interests, among others and the rise in unemployment, which was blamed on Puerto Rico's problem of "over population". U.S. policymakers determined that as, a policy course to address an excess of people, emigration would alleviate the situation. As a result, numerous expeditions were organized to send workers to other places, including the newly incorporated U.S. territory of Hawai'i (1900–1901). The effort conducted by private agencies to recruit and export workers was fraught with problems and inconsistencies forcing the local government to manage the exportation of laborers. In addition, after 1898, Puerto Ricans increasingly sought, through social and familial contacts, to migrate to cities like New York, Tampa and Philadelphia to settle among the earlier communities established by their predecessors (Whalen 2001: 10, 12).

The flow of Puerto Rican migrants to the U.S. and the permanent settlement of thousands established many informal networks that contributed to a continuation of migration and cemented community structures. These ethnic enclaves served the migrants by providing mutual aid, employment and housing information and a host of community support organizations that assisted the transition of Puerto Rican migrants to the U.S. The institutionalization of migration occurred as the formalization and elaboration of networks became independent of the factors that originally sparked migration (Massey et al. 1998: 42–3).

In 1917, the U.S. Congress passed the Jones Act which granted Puerto Ricans U.S. citizenship. Despite this change, it had no impact on the political status of the Island. However, with US citizenship, Puerto Ricans were able to travel more freely to the United States. After W.W. I, U.S. economic and political polices continued to have a significant impact on the Island by concentrating wealth in the hands of U.S. corporations and continuously displacing workers and creating conditions for emigration. For instance, between 1920 and 1940, the Puerto Rican population of the U.S. grew from 12,000 to 70,000. While the largest portion went to New York, a significant number of those migrants landed in Philadelphia.

Puerto Rico's economic dependence would grow in this time period as more and more cultivable land came under U.S. corporate control and more people were displaced. Most of this land came under the control of U.S sugar interests yet, there were a few Puerto Rican land owning families. The land dedicated to sugar cultivation increased dramatically from 72,146 to 145,433 acres between 1899 and 1909, and to 237,758 acres by 1929! (Whalen 2001: 13).

During the interwar period, network connections cemented the base of a community which provided for social identity, a way of behavior and a frequency of internal activity and dependence enclaves that evolved during the first decades of the twentieth century. Language, in this case Spanish, cultural identity and institutional development characterized the formation of a Puerto Rican enclave in Philadelphia as early as the 1920s. The intricate organizational network and leadership of these enclaves throughout the U.S. played a decisive role in the later development of U.S.-based Puerto Rican communities during the 1950s and 1960s (Hernández Álvarez 1968: 41).

The basic premise of the development of these communities is embodied in the concept of social capital described by Douglas Massey. Social capital is comprised of a combination of intangible resources in families and communities that help develop socially migrant networks. These networks serve to connect the current and former migration in Puerto Rico and the United States through family and friendship. Since the 1920s, these networks have been recognized as important in promoting and sustaining international migration. Social capital is also created when relations among persons change in ways that facilitate action. Massey argues that migration itself is a catalyst for social capital. The first Puerto Rican migrants had no contact therefore, for them migration was more costly. Those that followed did not find it as costly (Massey et al. 1998: 42–3).

During the period from 1910 to 1945, Puerto Ricans increasingly looked toward Philadelphia as a city of choice for migration. The reasons are very much linked to the island's colonial history and political and economic subjugation. The sugar industry, the island's primary export product under Spain in the nineteenth century, became absolutely dependent on its U.S. market after 1898. Also, the presence of Spanish-speaking communities in cities like Philadelphia attracted Puerto Rican migrants to many parts of the U.S. Given U.S. labor needs, Puerto Ricans increasingly became an important component of cheap labor sent to many parts of the States, thus dispersing Puerto Ricans throughout the country.

The economic and political changes in Puerto Rico during the pre-WW II years and the relatively direct transportation to the city facilitated this movement. Philadelphia's industrial base, especially its cigar manufacturing companies, provided additional incentives for Puerto Ricans to migrate to the city. In addition, the already existent Pan-Hispanic enclaves in Philadelphia, in formation since the end of the nineteenth century, also served to lure Puerto Ricans to the City. Although New York received the bulk of this migration, during the first decades of the twentieth century the city of Philadelphia had attracted sufficient numbers to have clearly defined settlements.

Between 1900 and 1945, more than 120,000 Puerto Ricans migrated to the United States. Fifty thousand of those arrived during World War II alone (1941–1945)—see Table 1. Most of them were concentrated in the Northeast and Midwestern regions of the country. The arrival of Puerto Ricans to Philadelphia marked a period of significant change for the city both in its regional economy and in its racial and ethnic composition. Though Philadelphia never attracted as many immigrants as cities like New York or Chicago, its immigrants did make up 25 percent of the city's total population by World War I. In addition, during this period, the city's black population also grew dramatically as the movement of African Americans from the South during World War I and II soared.

Table 1: Puerto Ricans (born in Puerto Rico) in United States Cities of Over 100,000 – 1910, 1920, and, 1940

	1910	1920	1940
New York City, NY	554	7,364	69,603
San Francisco, CA	213	474	603
Philadelphia, PA	64	319	440
Washington, DC	48	148	327
Chicago, IL	15	110	240
Baltimore, MD	44	91	231
Los Angeles	10	101	212
Oakland, CA	10	101	194
New Orleans, LA	15	177	153
Detroit, MI	4	59	153
Newark, NJ	5	22	198
Tampa, FL	64	94	123
Jersey City, NJ	3	56	106
Boston, MA	10	67	91
Buffalo, NY	12	56	106
Cleveland, OH	3	26	61
Yonkers, NY	1	13	55
San Antonio, TX	6	6	53
Houston, TX	0	3	50
St. Louis, MO	6	59	50

* Sources: Clarence O. Senior, *Puerto Rican Emigration*, (Rio Piedras, Puerto Rico: University of Puerto Rico, 1947, p. 45; U.S. Manuscript Census Population for 1910, 1920 and 1940

Many Puerto Ricans were also attracted to Philadelphia in these early decades by contacts made through informal networks developed by earlier migrants. These networks served to get the word out to the island of the existence of Spanish-speaking enclaves in the city as well as employment opportunities there. This was especially true for cigar makers, who were accustomed to traveling throughout the United States and the Caribbean in search of work. One example of this was Saturnino Dones (1881–1952), a Puerto Rican cigar maker and labor leader. Dones, who was active in the labor movement in Puerto Rico, settled in Philadelphia in 1902. At that time, the island was convulsed by political violence propagated mostly by members of the Puerto Rico Republican Party against labor organizers. Dones and many of his associates within the labor movement including Santiago Iglesias were forced to leave the island to avoid persecution. Another was Antonio Malpica. Malpica's motivation for moving is less clear. He could have been motivated by the changes taking place in the cigar industry on the island where women began to out-number men, leaving many of them unemployed. Also, the continuous business transactions between the island and Philadelphia, especially in the sphere of sugar and tobacco, contributed to promote the city as a point of attraction for Puerto Rican migrants. Communication between Puerto Rico, Cuba, New York, Tampa and Philadelphia among Spanish-speakers as well as the increased migration of Cubans and Spaniards to the city in the early twentieth century also helped consolidate the group into a Pan-Hispanic presence in the city. In addition, the recruitment efforts of companies such as the Pennsylvania Railroad Company also attracted Spanish-speaking workers to the region. Many of these migrants eventually settled in Philadelphia.

The many job opportunities for Puerto Rican migrants in this time period was complimented by the existence of a network of boarding houses near a number of work places where they toiled. This was particularly true for those who worked for heavy industries like the Baldwin Locomotive Works located in Spring Garden. Most Puerto Rican machinists who worked for Baldwin at the time were listed in the 1920 Manuscript Census as having arrived between 1917 and 1919. After the war Malpica, like Saturnino Dones and dozens of other Puerto Ricans continued to work in the city's major cigar manufacturing plants like the Bayuk Brothers, and continued to labor there during the 1930s and 40s.

Another smaller, but important segment of the migration was those who came to Philadelphia for business purposes or to study in many of the city's colleges and universities such as Jose DeCelis (1896–1961), Pedro Carreras (1892–1941) and Juan Pizarro, among others. These in particular, became part of the growing group of professionals and middle class. DeCelis arrived in 1915 and attended Temple University Dental School then located in the Spring Garden section of the City while Carreras who served in the Army during WW I and later became a doctor as did Juan Pizarro. All of them remained in Philadelphia and lived among other Puerto Ricans in the City. This group also included Mary Rodriguez (1906–1998), a schoolteacher and her husband Tomas (1905–1968), a pharmaceutical professional. Mary migrated to Philadelphia in 1931 and married Tomas that same year. Tomas Rodriguez had arrived two years earlier after his hometown friend Dr. Pedro Carreras wrote to him about a job in the pharmaceutical industry.[4]

Brief Historiography of the Early Puerto Rican Diaspora during the Interwar years

The literature on Puerto Ricans in the U.S. during the interwar period is quite limited. There is also a clear demarcation between the literature that has been produced in the United States by American scholars, with the exception of scholars like Ruth Glasser and Lorrin Thomas, and that written by Puerto Rican scholars, especially those of the second generation. For their part, many American scholars have focused almost exclusively on the experience of the post-World War II migrants emphasizing their "problems of adjustments" or, more recently as the other "crisis" group along with African Americans in the inner city. On the other hand, Puerto Rican scholars have added the factor of the political dependency relationship (colonialism) to their analysis, something most Americans have conveniently ignored. Also, a small but growing number of Puerto Rican scholars have begun to focus on the Puerto Rican presence in the pre-World War II period as one that provides missing ingredients to the overall analysis of the group's migratory experience in the U.S. Specifically, this pre-World War II historical analysis has shed important light on the experience of community building, cultural affirmation and political struggles of Puerto Ricans in the U.S. in the early years. This previously unknown or ignored chapter of the history of Puerto Ricans in the U.S. has come to call into question much of the analysis of American scholars regarding the internal functions of this ethnic group in the U.S. (Chenault 1938; Mills, Senior and Kohn Goldsen 1950: 23; Handlin 1959; Glazer and Moynihan 1970: 96, 102–3; Lewis 1965: xiii, xxviii).

Throughout the 1980s and 1990s, a few graduate students and other scholars augmented the production of works on the Puerto Rican experience in the United States. Utilizing the increasing manuscript collections amassed by the Center for Puerto Rican Studies library and Archives located in Hunter College, New York, these scholars produced a body literature by and about Puerto Ricans with the unique distinction of the ever growing and diverse emigrant experience. The literature on Puerto Rican migration in these years also began to reflect an integrated approach, examining the experience of the migrant along with those who remained on the island, as one community.[5]

Very few other Puerto Rican communities have been able to make the connection between the pre- and postwar period. The big exception has been New York City. Through the efforts of participants and scholars, fellow historians have been able to uncover, using a great many sources, and fill the gaps in the literature on the Puerto Rican experience in the U.S. Taken together as a collection, the works of Bernardo Vega, Virginia Sanchez-Korrol, Ruth Glasser and Lorrin Thomas present a portrait of a Puerto Rican community in New York City that between the war years had blossomed among other Hispanic and racial and ethnic minorities. These enclaves evolved over decades and taken together these four books have challenged the former conventional wisdom that denied its very existence. They have a direct relevance to my study of the Puerto Rican experience in Philadelphia because they provide comparative measures against which readers can relate the experience of Puerto Ricans in Philadelphia and New York.

In the mid-1970s, the writings of Puerto Rico cigar maker Bernardo Vega were "re-discovered" when his memoirs were published. First produced in Spanish by Ediciones Huracán, in Puerto Rico. *Memorias de Bernardo Vega: contribución a la historia de la comunidad puertorriqueña en Nueva York* (1975), edited by Cesar Andreu Iglesias. These were subsequently published in English as *Memoirs of Bernardo Vega: A Contribution to the History of the Puerto Rican community in New York* (1984) and edited by U.S. Puerto Rican scholar Juan Flores is a quasi-biographical account of Vega's life from the time he left Puerto Rico in 1916 and settled in New York, until his return to the Island in 1948. The publication of Vega's memoir was one of the most important books of this period because it documented, in the voice of someone who had lived the experience, the presence of a Puerto Rican community in the United States in the early period. Vega's rich detail of everyday life of Puerto Rican workers in New York City especially cigar makers, provided a rare view from the perspectives of blue-collar workers. Although focused on New York City and the development of that community in the first forty years of the twentieth century, Vega's memoir corroborates the presence of Puerto Rican communities in other cities, especially Philadelphia and Boston (Vega 1977).

Vega's *Memoirs*, more than just a chronicle of Puerto Rican migration and the experience of the emigrant community in the United States, also provides a more complete theoretical understanding of the impact of U.S. capitalism and colonialism on his beloved island. Contrarily, very few American scholars who have written on the subject of the Puerto Rican experience in the United States in the post-World War II period touch upon the subject of colonialism. The most significant contribution of Bernardo Vega's *Memoirs,* however, is best summarized in the English translation of the manuscript by Juan Flores, who wrote in the preface arguing that the value of the memoir was the dispelling of the myth that Puerto Ricans were newcomers in the 1950s. Rather, argued Flores, the memoir is living proof of the existence of a Puerto Rican community in New York during the inter war period (Flores 1984: ix–x).

Further historical research on the presence of Puerto Ricans in the pre-World War II period made a significant contribution to the literature and methodologies utilized in community studies. These benefited from the work of the Center for Puerto Rican Studies, especially its vast and growing archival manuscript collections, which would be used to expand the narrative that Vega's *Memoirs* described. One of the original members of the Center's History Task Force in the mid-1970s was Virginia Sánchez-Korrol, at the time, a doctoral student at Old Westbury College at the State University of New York (SUNY) in Long Island. In 1983, Sánchez-Korrol published her revised dissertation, *From Colonia to Community: The History of Puerto Ricans in New York City, 1917–1948.* The book deals with the Puerto Rican community in New York City during a similar time period as the one depicted by Bernardo Vega's *Memoirs,* mostly the interwar years. Sánchez-Korrol was prompted by the experiences of her own family, which migrated from the island in the 1920s. In the preface of the book, Sánchez-Korrol describes the project in this way "Unable to reconcile the available writings on Puerto Ricans with my own memories of a *colonia* soundly structured by strict family values, a concern for cultural heritage, and an identifiable organizational network. . I embarked on a search which led to. . . the writing of this book." Sanchez Korrol subsequently updated this book in a second edition (1997) she added a chapter which connected with the Great Migration experience in New York City (Sánchez-Korrol 1994: vii).

Utilizing a virtually unknown mid-decennial 1925 New York State Manuscript Census for Assembly Districts 16–19 (Spanish Harlem) located in the New York City Hall Records as well as records of numerous organizations in the Spanish-speaking enclaves in the city, Sanchez-Korrol was able to confirm and expand upon the description of a thriving Puerto Rican community during the inter-war years which Bernardo Vega himself had experienced. Sánchez-Korrol stressed that the political and economic conditions on the island, that prompted this early migratory wave was impacted by the colonial status of Puerto Rico. She also thoroughly examined the process of institutional development of the Puerto Rican community during this period. Curiously, American scholars such as Lawrence Chenault, Oscar Handlin, Clarence Senior and Nathan Glazer and Daniel P. Moynihan who wrote about the Puerto Rican migration experience in the 1930s, 50s and 60s did not "discover," much less utilize these rich primary sources, in their works. Sánchez-Korrol's study made an important contribution to the historical study of Puerto Ricans in the use of her methodology; especially the use of oral histories and manuscript census material which documented the very community negated by earlier scholars (Sánchez-Korrol 1994: chapter 2).

The work of public historian Ruth Glasser's *My Music is My Flag: Puerto Rican Musicians and Their New York Communities, 1917–1940* (1995) and *Aquí Me Quedo: Puerto Ricans in Connecticut/Los Puertorriqueños en Connecticut* (1997), are two publications that have made a contribution in connecting the pre- and post-World War II

Puerto Rican migration outside of New York (Connecticut). In *My Music Is My Flag*, Glasser discusses, in depth, the rich diversity of Puerto Rican musicians in the U.S. musical scene of the interwar period. Glasser contributes, with this monograph, an additional criticism of the view that Puerto Ricans were "weak in folk arts unsure in its cultural traditions, [and] without a powerful faith," directed, in particular, at such early American scholars like Glazer and Moynihan's views of Puerto Ricans. Thus, *My Music is My Flag* has become, along with Bernardo Vega's *Memoirs* and Sánchez-Korrol's *From Colonia to Community*, a powerful voice that calls into question the myriad of studies on Puerto Ricans that not only focus on the social problems of this group but that collectively view these migrants through a crisis-oriented lens in contemporary literature. More importantly, Glasser's analysis adds to our understanding of early Puerto Rican contributions to American society by arguing that "both their presence and their music injected new variables into a society accustomed to thinking in dichotomies of black and white, ethnic and assimilated." In fact, argues Glasser, "the history of the careers of these musicians challenges the typical ethnic-to-American stereotypes." This group also includes the fine work by historian Lorrin Thomas, who's *Puerto Rican Citizen: History and Political Identity in Twentieth-Century New York City* (2010), raises the age old question of what is U.S. Citizenship for Puerto Ricans in the process of community building of migrants from a U.S. Colony. The duality of being *foreigners* and *citizens* at the same time is aptly argued by Thomas in this path breaking study. Together these community studies have gone a long way toward dispelling the notions that Puerto Ricans in the United States had no community structures or institutions in the pre-Great Migration Era.

This book also situates Puerto Rican migration to Philadelphia within a global economic context during the course of the twentieth-century. The significant increase of the Puerto Rican presence in Philadelphia was a direct consequence of the Island's passing from Spanish to American colonial control at the end of the nineteenth century. The impact of the American presence on the Island was felt immediately after the Spanish-American War in 1898. As American interests took hold of the island, economic and social relations were upset by the new political order, leading to widespread unemployment. The economic sectors most affected by the American occupation were the coffee, sugar and tobacco industries which employed most Puerto Ricans at the time. Puerto Rican migration needs to be seen as an example of a labor migration from the periphery to the core country; it is important to explore the structural factors behind migration.

Another important aspect of the Philadelphia migration is the role played by informal networks. Informal networks fostered the expansion of Pan-Hispanic enclaves in the city, as Puerto Rican migrants settled near their compatriots. During the early decades of the twentieth century neighborhoods like Spring Garden, Northern Liberties, and Southwark in South Philadelphia were known for their multi-ethnic composition (Pajil 1999; Santiago 1994).

Between 1914 and 1919, Puerto Rican migration to Philadelphia contributed to the expansion of the Pan-Hispanic enclaves in the city. One important reason for the increase in Puerto Rican migration to the U.S. was the existence of these enclaves in cities like New York and Philadelphia. Some Puerto Ricans like Thomas Guiannol and Christian Martinez came to work in WW I defense industries (U.S. Department of Commerce 1920). Others came to study at Temple University, the University of Pennsylvania, among others. This early migration to the city, this study describes, was consequential in the further development and expansion of these enclaves during the 1920's and 1930's. A review of manuscript census data for 1910 through 1940 demonstrates that the clustering of Puerto Ricans in the Spring Garden, Northern Liberties and Southwark sections of the city in this time period was especially significant. Within these settlements informal networks developed, which in turn, contributed to attracting more Puerto Rican migrants to the city. Out of this process, a new ethnic community gradually developed. During the first half of the twentieth century these enclaves were both ethnic and working-class as well as containing a smattering of a small middle class.[6] This professional class included, in addition to Drs. DeCelis and Carreras, individuals like Mary and Tomas Rodríguez, the Reverend Enrique Rodriguez, and his wife, Tomasita, a teacher; and Domingo Martinez who arrived in the early 1940s as well as the priests of La Milagrosa (Our Lady of the Miraculous Medal chapel) the first catholic Spanish language church in Philadelphia (1909). Led by individuals such as these, the Pan-Hispanic settlements eventually became the Puerto Rican community of today. These individuals played an important formative role in that community.

On a cold, windy but sunny afternoon in March 7, 1999, 90-year-old Mary Rodriguez sat in her West Mt. Airy kitchen in the house in which she lived with her daughter Emma and recounted how she and her deceased husband Tomas arrived in Philadelphia during the Great Depression. In the early 1930s, Tomás Rodriguez came to Philadelphia from Puerto Rico when a hometown friend, Pedro Carreras, told him about a job at a local pharmaceutical company in the city. Like other Puerto Ricans, his migration can be understood as part of a labor migration shaped by networks that had begun to develop among Puerto Rican migrants in the City. At the time he learned about this job opportunity, Tomás had been working at the local drugstore in his hometown of Juana Diaz, located in the southern part of the island. He had begun studies as a pharmacist but because of limited funds, had not completed them. The chance to go to Philadelphia offered Rodriguez the possibility of not only a job but also of completing his studies. His friend in Philadelphia, Dr. Pedro Carreras, lived on North 5th Street in the Northern Liberties section of the city, where a Spanish-speaking enclave had begun to evolve. Carreras thus formed part of an informal network of Puerto Ricans that promoted the city and lured other migrants. Carreras, who had served in the US Army during WW I, had studied medicine in Philadelphia and stayed on after completing his studies (Rodríguez 1999; Martínez 1923).[7]

This book also compares the residential and occupational experiences of Puerto Ricans with that of Philadelphia's major racial and ethnic groups of the period. The employment and housing patterns of Puerto Ricans and other Latinos in the interwar period is compared with that of "native-born whites," "foreign-born whites" and "blacks" (African Americans), the major categories utilized by the U.S. Census Bureau at that time. Similarities and differences among these groups indicate that during the first half of the twentieth century, there were distinctive characteristics exhibited by the residential and occupational patterns between Puerto Ricans and the rest of the population of Philadelphia. This pattern would continue into the second half of the century as Philadelphia experienced a process of deindustrialization and of "white flight."

Networks continued to shape the migration to Philadelphia, with some Puerto Ricans coming via New York City. When Tomas Rodriguez moved to Philadelphia for work he was already courting Mary. However, she never received a letter from him. While Tomas kept writing to her and not getting a response. This was all due to shenanigans at Mary's local post office where his letters were intercepted due to some family feud. In the meantime, Mary, believing Tomas had forgotten about her arranged to visit her Aunt "Ita" who lived in New York City during the Easter break in 1931. When Mary Rodriguez arrived in New York City in 1931, Tomás Rodriguez was waiting for her on the pier. Although he lived in Philadelphia, at the time, Tomas, who knew Aunt Ita and visited her found out that Mary was coming to NY. Upon learning that his sweetheart was going to be in New York, he showed up to meet her at the pier. Mary had planned to be in New York for only a short vacation because she had to return to her job as a schoolteacher in Puerto Rico where she was still under contract. Tomás Rodriguez, however, had other plans. They married right away and Tomás Rodriguez moved his new bride to his apartment located in the Spring Garden neighborhood in a Spanish-speaking settlement in Philadelphia. Another Puerto Rican who came to the City through New York was Domingo Martinez, who would become a well-established businessman in Philadelphia and leader of the Puerto Rican community in the 1950s. He had lived in New York City with his brother since his arrival from Puerto Rico in 1936. Others, like Juan Canales, came to Philadelphia in 1944 searching for his home town friend, Marcelino Benitez and a job. Benitez had written to Canales about a job the Campbell Soup Company located in Camden, New Jersey just across the river from the city of Philadelphia (Pajil 1999; Rodríguez 1999; Canales 1999) .

Puerto Ricans did not, however, live in isolation. Those who migrated to Phila-delphia in the interwar period often shared residential space with other immigrant or migrant groups. Prominent among these were the Italians and the Polish. Together with Russian Jews, Italians and Polish made up the bulk of the "new" immigrants who arrived in Philadelphia in large numbers at the turn of the twentieth century. African Americans, who migrated from the South during the early twentieth century, also comprised a large migrant group with whom Puerto Ricans shared communal space. A comparison with these groups sheds light into how Puerto Ricans fared as the social and racial composition of Philadelphia shifted in the first half of the of the twentieth century and became the genesis of the racial conflicts encountered by Puerto Ricans who arrived in the City after WW II.

Finally, this book carries the analysis of the strides early Puerto Ricans took to include another major city, Philadelphia, to the expanding study of this little known community. Hopefully, this study will be a contribution that will help fill the gap of ethnic and immigration studies in Philadelphia, such as those by Allen F. Davis and Mark Haller; Theodore Hershberg, Carolyn Adams, and others. These studies high-light the relationship between ethnic and racial groups in the city, however; there is little or no mention of Puerto Ricans or any Spanish-speaking immigrant group in Philadelphia. Davis and Haller's anthology, *The Peoples of Philadelphia* (1976), for ex-ample, does not mention Spanish-speakers at all, while Hershberg, Adams, et al, and Judith Goode and Joanne Schneider only refer to Puerto Ricans or Hispanics in the post-World War II period. This study begins to help fill this lacuna (Davis and Heller 1976; Hershberg et al. 1981; Adams et al. 1991; Goode and Schneider 1994: chapter 2).

The following chapters provide a fuller discussion of the themes presented in this introduction. In Chapter 2, I discuss the reasons why Puerto Ricans progressive-ly looked toward Philadelphia as a place to migrate by examining the links they de-veloped that continuously promoted the city as place to go to. It provides an overview of how Philadelphia became a hub for political activists from Puerto Rico during the mid- to late nineteenth century. This chapter explores the role of informal networks and labor migration connections in attracting migrants to the industrial base of the city and the cigar making industry and its global connection to Puerto Rican migration to Philadelphia. In addition, in this chapter I also articulate how and why the existent Pan-Hispanic enclaves, existent in Philadelphia since the late nineteenth century, lured Puerto Ricans during a period of significant changes in the economic life of the City while adding to the diversity of Spanish-speaking Philadelphia.

In Chapter 3, I explore how Puerto Ricans in Philadelphia in the early decades of the twentieth century went from living dispersed throughout the City forming and developing their respective settlements within the changing racial and ethnic composition of Philadelphia at that time. Puerto Rican migrants arriving in the City during those interwar years were impacted by the dramatic population shift in the city at the time, and I point to the development of residential patterns among Puerto Ricans that had more in common with those of African Americans who were the most segregated group in the city. This chapter also reviews housing patterns in Philadelphia during the 1920s and 30s and the residential patterns of the Pan-Hispanic enclaves, patterns that influenced where many Puerto Rican migrants settled after 1945.

In Chapter 4, I look more closely at the occupational patterns of Puerto Ricans in Philadelphia during the first half of the twentieth century with special emphasis on the interwar years. I also examine economic conditions before WW II as well as its impact on workers on the Island, an influence that prompted and promoted migration to the U.S. This chapter also outlines how Puerto Rican workers: blue-collar, white-collar and professionals reflected similarities with other foreign-born workers. This class structure is compared to African Americans, Foreign-born whites and Native-born white workers. I end the chapter by arguing how, by the end of World War II, Puerto Ricans' job opportunities and employment patterns in the city began to resemble more that of African Americans than any other major migrant or ethnic group in Philadelphia at the time. Furthermore, this chapter discusses how Puerto Rican migration during WW II and labor recruitment of wartime workers to the region helped shape a Puerto Rican community in the City.

The social patterns developed by the Pan-Hispanic colonias during the interwar years served as the groundwork for the evolution of a full-fledged Puerto Rican community in Philadelphia. In chapter 5, I explore the community efforts of the three main Spanish-speaking enclaves of Spring Garden, Northern Liberties and Southwark and how they formed a compact community in Philadelphia by the end of World War II. The early arrival of Puerto Ricans enhanced the small but significant organizational network of mutual aid, labor and other social organizations and helped to broaden these Pan-Hispanic enclaves.

Lastly, the Epilogue explores how the legacies bequeathed by the early migrants impacted the "Great" migration of Puerto Ricans led to racial clashes which took place in Spring Garden in the summer of 1953 which contributed to the City's recognition of a "Puerto Rican" Problem and other defining moments in the early development of the Puerto Rican community in the 1950s and 1960s. It analyzes the turbulent progress of the Puerto Rican community in Philadelphia during the 1950s through the 1980s by examining the rise of second generation community struggles and the impact of the Civil Rights movement on the community. I also look at the election of Puerto Ricans to local and state office and the increase of community based organizations. The chapter also examines the changes in Latino Philadelphia as many different Latino groups migrated to the city beginning in the 1990s and the increasing transformation into a more Pan-Latino community, although as of this writing, Puerto Ricans in Philadelphia still make up about 60 percent of Latinos in the City.

CHAPTER 2

Puerto Rican Migration to Philadelphia: An Overview

Introduction

The cause of Puerto Rican migration to Philadelphia during the latter part of the nineteenth and first half of the twentieth century reflected the economic and political shifts that occurred in Puerto Rico especially after the U.S. takeover in 1898. Initially, Puerto Rican political activists trying to free the island from Spanish control during the nineteenth century viewed Philadelphia as a friendly place to plot their insurgency. After the struggle for the independence of Cuba and Puerto Rico dissolved in 1898, the settlements established during that political era became very important in attracting Puerto Rican migrants to the city especially cigar makers. Between 1898 and 1945, Philadelphia became, after New York, the recipient of ever greater numbers of Puerto Ricans. In cementing their presence in the city, Pan-Hispanic enclaves also developed important organizations which helped to stabilize and provide an important cultural and religious connection for new migrants. Friends of Puerto Ricans, who resided in Philadelphia wrote back home about job opportunities and, as in the case of Tomás Rodriguez and Juan Canales, specific jobs for them. Prompted by the economic and political environment on the island and by people in the networks and by the city's continued need for labor, first hundreds and then thousands of Puerto Ricans migrated to Philadelphia. The commercial, political and labor connections between Puerto Ricans and the city of Philadelphia was a contributing factor for their choice of settling in the City.

As an important port city, Philadelphia has played a pivotal role in the history of the United States. As a major economic hub, the City has also experienced significant immigration since the dawn of the Republic. The evolution of commerce throughout the nineteenth century and the political upheaval in the Americas during that time established Philadelphia as a central recipient of immigrants from Latin America and the Caribbean, especially from Cuba and Puerto Rico.

The migration of Puerto Ricans to Philadelphia in the nineteenth century was caused by three factors: economic ties between Philadelphia and the island; revolutionary activity among Puerto Ricans who used the city of Philadelphia as a base of operations for their anti-Spanish endeavors; and labor migrants, especially cigar makers, who progressively found in the Philadelphia cigar making industry employment security. Cigar makers were revolutionaries and labor migrants at the same time. They also contributed to the diversification of the Pan-Hispanic settlements in the City.

At the dawn of the nineteenth century, events in Europe beginning with the Napoleonic wars had a ripple effect on the Spanish Empire in the Americas and the Caribbean. The invasion of Spain by France (1804) wreaked havoc on the Spanish colonial enterprise and began to cripple the colonial structures across the New World. Coupled with reforms that the Spanish authorities implemented in the Americas. This led to, for the first time, the *Criollos,* the local Latin American elites of Spanish descent, to increase their political strength. The ascent of the local elites eventually led to the Latin American independence movements. Encouraged by the American colonists' defeat of Great Britain and the establishment of the United States of America, the Spanish and Caribbean colonies saw the nascent republic not only as a model but as a potential ally. Many prominent U.S. port cities became hubs of political intrigue where exiles conspired to achieve independence from Spain and sought support for their respective causes. Also, as the United States consolidated its economy, Americans sought to expand trade with Latin America and the Caribbean. In the case of Puerto Rico, as we will see, this economic relation became more regularized and created the migratory patterns north, especially to port cities like Philadelphia.

As one-by-one the Latin American colonies achieved their independence from Spain, by 1825, the former empire had been reduced to only two possessions in the Caribbean: Cuba and Puerto Rico. In order to maintain control and hold on to its last vestiges of its imperial power, Spain undertook increasingly more repressive measures and other mechanisms of social control on both islands. The economy of the islands still under Spanish control sought to make the colonial enterprise still profitable by allowing for greater trade with the "neutral" United States. Thus, inadvertently promoting the creation of commercial and migratory patterns to emerge and that would only increase throughout the nineteenth century.

The origins of Puerto Rican migration to Philadelphia lay in the eighteenth century. Ships from the island brought sugar and molasses to the city, goods sought by merchants from all over Pennsylvania. During the nineteenth-century, trade between the United States and Puerto Rico, especially through the port of Philadelphia, was brisk. This expansion in trade opened the doors to migration, albeit in small numbers (Sánchez-Korrol 1994: 9, 12). By 1807, vessels from Philadelphia were making regular stops in Puerto Rico. In that same year, an American consular agent was appointed to the island, no doubt a sign of the increase importance in the commercial relationship.

The War of 1812 interrupted commercial trade between the U.S. and Puerto Rico, but once the war ended in 1815, trade picked up again (Morales Carrión 1984: 63).[1]

Throughout the nineteenth century, Puerto Rican revolutionary activity in Philadelphia created another important connection to the island. For example, in 1822 an armed expedition equipped for the purpose of invading Puerto Rico and link up with Puerto Rican conspirators bent on liberating the island from Spain was outfitted in Philadelphia. The voyage, led by Louis Du Coudray Holstein, a German-French soldier of fortune who had collaborated with the Latin American liberator Simon Bolivar, however, it was captured in Curacao when the ship, due to bad weather, was forced to land at the Dutch colony located off the coast of Venezuela (Morales Carríon 1984: 76).[2]

In addition to Puerto Ricans, Philadelphia also attracted other Spanish-speakers, which contributed to the expansion of the growing enclave. In 1823, Father Felix Varela y Morales, an exiled anti-Spanish, Cuban Catholic priest, arrived in Philadelphia and settled among the Spanish speaking residents of the City. He spent two years in the city where he founded and edited *El Habanero*, the first Spanish language newspaper to be published in Philadelphia. Varela had been a professor of Philosophy at the San Carlos and San Antonio Seminaries in Havana. In 1821, he was elected as a Cuban representative to the Spanish Cortes. However, when the Cortes was abolished by royal decree in 1823, Varela, an outspoken advocate for Cuban freedom, sought refuge in the United States. Through his writings in *El Habanero* he continued to champion the cause of Cuban independence. Although Varela lived in Philadelphia for a short time, his presence and editing of *El Habanero* contributed to the small but growing Spanish-speaking presence in the city (Dolan and Vidal 1994: 162; Connelly 1976: 593; McCadden and McCadden 1969: 38–72; Willging and Hatzfeld 1968: 69–70; *The New Catholic Encyclopedia* 2002: 539).[3]

Once most Spanish colonies in Latin America achieved their independence, many of their former colonial elites migrated to Puerto Rico and Cuba: the last remnants of the Spanish empire on the American continent. Although their presence on these islands contributed to a dampening of pro-independence sentiment, by the 1850s revolutionary fervor had once again been ignited in Puerto Rico. Several of these anti-colonial movements were organized and carried out from bases in the United States. Philadelphia, New York, Boston, New Orleans among other cities became hubs of revolutionary activity. These revolutionary movements advocated the independence of both islands. In the mid-1860s, Puerto Rican and Cuban exiles living in the United States once again stoked the flames of revolution in the Caribbean. The Philadelphia Spanish-speaking enclave was very much involved in these activities (Delgado Pasapera 1984: 105).

Other examples of Puerto Rican revolutionary activity in the city of Philadelphia in this time period were the different projects that involved the unity of political purpose of liberating the island along with those of the island of Cuba. By mid-century, Puerto Ricans and Cubans in Philadelphia began to unite their efforts in the cause for the independence of both islands. In 1865, they jointly organized a local chapter of the Republican Society of Cuba and Puerto Rico. The central leadership was headquartered in New York. Among the undertakings of this group, the Society collaborated with the insurgents on the islands of Cuba and Puerto Rico when in 1868 they launched their respective struggles for independence (Delgado Pasapera 1984: 106).[4]

The political situation in Puerto Rico during the second half of the nineteenth century continued to connect Philadelphia and the Spanish-Speaking Caribbean. Political activism among Puerto Ricans who resided in the United States, especially in Philadelphia, began to take shape with the arrival of Dr. José Francisco Basora in New York City in 1860. Dr. Basora, a Puerto Rican revolutionary who had been an active member of the island's abolitionist movement since the 1850s, had been studying medicine in France. Together with Dr. Ramón Emeterio Betances, another Puerto Rican abolitionist and premier revolutionary, Basora worked for the cause of Puerto Rican independence for the next thirty years; he was a fervent organizer. He was one of the two Vice Presidents of the Republican Society of Cuba and Puerto Rico. Not a lot is known about this Society's work in the City, but the mere fact of its existence in Philadelphia also attests to the importance given to the Spanish-speaking hub in the city by the group in New York as well as on the island. Clearly, with Basora in the leadership the outreach to Philadelphia surely helped to develop stronger ties between the revolutionaries in both cities. This most certainly served to attract more Puerto Ricans to the city (Delgado Passapera 1984: 107).

By the early 1890s, the tobacco industry in Philadelphia was very strong. Utilizing imported leaves from Cuba and Puerto Rico among other places in the Caribbean, the city's industries produced some of the finest cigars. Philadelphia had more than 1,000 factories of which 136 of them employed at least 10 or more rollers each. A few of the major companies were entirely or partially owned by Cubans and Spaniards, these included the Juan F. Portuondo, Antonio Roig & Langsdorf and the Gray, Morales & Dalton Company. Spanish-speakers were also well represented among Philadelphia's cigar makers and cigar manufacturers. It was from this same occupational base that Cuban patriot and revolutionary leader, José Martí organized his U.S.-based Partido Revolucionario Cubano (PRC) [Cuban Revolutionary Party], which became the political arm of *Cuba Libre*, the Cuban national liberation movement of the late nineteenth century. From its bases in the United States, this movement helped launch the Cuban war for independence in 1895.

The PRC was founded in Tampa in 1892 and established its headquarters in New York City. In Philadelphia, Cubans and Puerto Ricans also united under Marti's leadership. From 1895 until 1898, when the United States invaded Cuba, the PRC served as the main support of the fighting units of the Cuban insurgents known as the *"mambises"* (Cigar Makers History in Philadelphia, PA n.d.).[5]

By 1892, local Cuban and Puerto Rican exiles in Philadelphia had formed six clubs of the Partido Revolucionario Cubano (PRC). The fact that the political platform of the PRC established a clear commitment with the cause of Puerto Rican independence prompted many islanders to join the cause. Philadelphia thus became the third most important city in support of Cuban and Puerto Rican independence in the United States behind those of New York and Tampa.[6]

Cigar makers were an important group which contributed a significant number of Puerto Rican migrants to Philadelphia during the late nineteenth century and early twentieth century. Throughout the second half of the nineteenth century, cigar makers migrated to the principal centers of cigar manufacturing in the United States. Amongst these centers were Tampa, Philadelphia, New Orleans and New York (Delgado Pasapera 1984; Vega 1984). Cigar makers, many of whom were political activists, were well known for their keen sense of organization. They founded some of the earliest Spanish-speaking mutual aid societies in the United States.[7] Another important role that cigar makers played was evident in the labor movement. Cigar makers played a pivotal role in the development of late nineteenth-century labor movements in the United States, Cuba and Puerto Rico. As early as 1877, cigar makers had established a Spanish-speaking local of the Cigar Makers International Union (CMIU) in Philadelphia.[8]

Local political organizing of the PRC in Philadelphia helped galvanize support in the region for the Cuban cause. More importantly, the breadth and depth of the PRC in Philadelphia energized the Spanish-speaking population and rallied, not only Cubans, to the cause but, Puerto Ricans and other Spanish-speakers as well. In New York, Puerto Ricans followed suit and organized their own section within the PRC. As the PRC extended its action to Philadelphia, Puerto Rican and Cuban revolutionaries found fertile ground for their economic and political endeavors in the industrial city (Vega 1984: 64). The membership of the PRC in Philadelphia included cigar makers and cigar manufacturers as well as laborers and professionals amongst its ranks (*Patria* 1898).

Between 1892 and 1898, Philadelphia was a hub of activity led by the PRC affiliates. The leadership was made up of some professionals, but most of its members were cigar makers.[9] Together, the PRC hosted many activities such as the dinner that was held in Philadelphia in 1892 in honor of José Martí. During this period, Marti visited Philadelphia on more than one occasion to speak before groups of Puerto Rican and Cuban residents. Not only did these revolutionaries launch a movement that nearly defeated Spain in Cuba, but they also succeeded, in the case of Philadelphia, in contributing to the formation of a clearly defined Spanish-speaking presence in the city especially in the Southwark area (*Patria* 1892; Vega 1984: 64).

In December 1898, in the aftermath of the Spanish-Cuban-American War, PRC officials disbanded the organization. Notwithstanding this action, however, a vibrant Spanish-speaking enclave remained and continued to develop in Philadelphia. Veterans of the PRC campaigns in the city helped to lead this community in its future development effort. As more Puerto Ricans continued to arrive in Philadelphia in the early years of the twentieth century, they connected with the earlier pioneers, especially those in the cigar making industry as they established roots in the city.[10]

Since the middle of the nineteenth century, U.S. cigar making and the tobacco industry generally, had had an important connection to these industries in Puerto Rico and Cuba. Concurrently, cigar makers in the states and on these islands shared an organizational, social and political vision. During the first two decades of the twentieth century, Puerto Rican cigar makers played a key role in the fundamental changes that occurred in their society. During this twenty-year period, the island became totally incorporated into the American economy. This absorption was most evident in the expansion of export agriculture based mostly on sugar and tobacco. Cigar makers rose to prominence in this time period. Their labor militancy led to numerous strikes as a measure of dealing with the enormous transformation that took place on the island in this era. When the political situation on the island got very difficult cigar makers, especially labor militants, often traveled to the states where their American brethren helped them secure employment. That is how many Puerto Rican cigar makers found jobs in the Philadelphia tobacco industry. [11]

An example of the early impact of the United States' presence on the island and its consequential relationship to migration to Philadelphia was on the tobacco industry and in particular cigar making. Cigar making on the Island, initially a male dominated and an artisan focused industry, was transformed in a few short decades into a female dominated, assembly line production that progressively incorporated new technology (machines) into the production of cigars. The end result of this manufacturing evolution led to two important changes in the industry: 1) the displacement of men from cigar making thereby, inducing migration of Puerto Rican male cigar makers like Antonio Malpica to cities like Philadelphia; and 2) the increasing incorporation of women into employment through factory-style cigar making.

In the early twentieth century, many Puerto Ricans were also attracted to Phila-delphia by contacts made through informal networks developed by earlier migrants, which alerted potential migrants to the Spanish-speaking presence in the city and to employment opportunities. The continuous business transactions between the is-land and Philadelphia, especially in the sphere of sugar and tobacco, contributed to promote the city as a point of attraction for Puerto Ricans. Communication between Puerto Rico, New York, Tampa and Philadelphia among Puerto Ricans also helped to expand migration patterns during this time period.

The changes that occurred in the tobacco industry between 1898 and 1930 radi-cally changed the composition of the Puerto Rican workforce dedicated to cigar mak-ing. Many male cigar makers chose the road of migration as a way of dealing with their displacement from what had been, for more than a half a century, one of their privileged domains. As many male cigar makers were displaced from their livelihood they sought other opportunities in the United States. It is difficult to say just how many Puerto Rican cigar makers migrated to the United States in this period, but judging from the accounts of Bernardo Vega in his memoirs, at the very least their presence was numerous and their labor participation and union activism in the Unit-ed States is legendary (Vega 1984).

War and the imposition of U.S. citizenship on Puerto Ricans in 1917 also had a tremendous impact on the movement of Puerto Ricans to the states (Sánchez-Korrol 1994: 18–9; Centro de Estudios Puertorriqueños 1982: 4–5). Migration of laborers also became an attractive policy for American officials on the island. The large num-bers of idle workers due largely to the seasonal nature of sugar and tobacco produc-tion alarmed the local authorities. The problem of surplus population, according to the U.S. colonial administration on the Island, reached crisis proportions during this time period. Hence, to deal with this "population" surplus it was recommended that, given the labor shortage in the United States, Puerto Ricans be contracted to fill many of the unskilled jobs that were available on the mainland during W.W. I (Centro de Estudios Puertorriqueños 1982: 5).

U.S. newspapers at the time carried reports of the impending need to bring Puerto Ricans as cheap labor to work for American railroad companies and on ag-ricultural farms (New York Times 1918; Centro de Estudios Puertorriqueños 1982: section II).[12] This was especially true for the Philadelphia region. It is estimated that during WW I, the U.S. War Department and the Bureau of Insular Affairs col-laborated in bringing more than 13,000 Puerto Ricans to work in the United States in defense industries; some were assigned to build military installations. The impact of this labor recruitment effort was that the Puerto Rican population in Philadelphia, though smaller than the one in New York City, grew consistently during World War I (Centro de Estudios Puertorriqueños 1979: 111).

It is difficult to determine the exact number of Puerto Ricans involved in these migratory movements but, judging from numbers provided by the U.S. Department of Justice, Immigration and Naturalization records covering the years between 1914 and 1920, Puerto Rico experienced a net loss of 12,356 residents during that time. For Philadelphia, this increase can be observed in the Spring Garden section of the city where a significant Pan-Hispanic enclave existed at the time. Data from the 1920 U.S. Manuscript Census reveals that many of the Puerto Rican migrants that arrived in Philadelphia during the World War I years; eighty-five percent did so between 1914 and 1919, with 65 percent having arrived between 1917 and 1919. Overall, the Puerto Rican population in Philadelphia grew five-fold between 1910 and 1920 (U.S. Department of Commerce 1920).

Not all Puerto Ricans who came to Philadelphia in the early decades of the twentieth century did so as laborers; some, as indicated earlier came for academic reasons: to study. One such case was that of Jose DeCelis, who arrived in 1915 at the age of nineteen. DeCelis came to Philadelphia to study at the School of Dentistry at Temple University. DeCelis, who originated from the southern city of Ponce, went to live in Spring Garden, where he resided for almost fifty years. The time span of his residence in the City of Brotherly Love marked the crucial stages of the establishment, settlement and development of the present day Puerto Rican community in Philadelphia. When DeCelis graduated from temple in 1918, he remained in Philadelphia until his death in 1961. DeCelis would surface along with other professionals as an important leader in the Puerto Rican community during World War II.

During the 1920s, the upward trend in Puerto Rican migration to the United States continued. Northeastern states like New York, New Jersey and Pennsylvania accounted for the bulk of this flow. One aspect of Puerto Rican migration to the United States in this period was prompted by the actions taken by local Puerto Rican authorities on the island to "manage" the migratory process. For instance, in 1919, the Puerto Rican government attempted to regulate migration, especially that of contracted laborers. Previous contract labor migrations had produced less than desirable effects. Many laborers had complained about the treatment by contractors as well as regarding the work and living conditions. This was also true among Puerto Ricans that were contracted to work on military installations during W.W. I. On May 29, 1919, the territorial legislature of Puerto Rico enacted a law in an effort to regulate emigration from the Island. This was an attempt to control the language and conditions of the contracts that were signed between potential Puerto Rican migrants and their respective employers, who were mostly Americans, but also included some foreign companies. The law established rules and punishment for violators, especially for the contractors. The local government used this law as a way of promoting migration under contracts (Centro de Estudios Puertorriqueños 1982: 140–1).

Some Puerto Ricans who came to Philadelphia in the 1920s and 1930s initially migrated to the agricultural areas of southern New Jersey. In the early 1920s, Puerto Rican agricultural workers arrived on farms in southern New Jersey to work picking tomatoes and other fruits. These were some of the early pioneers in that part of the state. Subsequently, the prevailing economic conditions in Puerto Rico during this period and the expansion of industrial jobs in Philadelphia attracted a growing number of these same Puerto Ricans to the city. Some Puerto Rican migrants, however, remained in the Vineland area and subsequently founded a Puerto Rican settlement there (Perez 1998: 80).[13]

Another flow of Puerto Rican migrants came from the South, particularly from the cigar making areas of Tampa and Key West, Florida. During the 1920s, the decline of the cigar industry, especially in cities like Tampa, prompted Puerto Ricans and Cubans to migrate north. In the 1920s, cigar-making machines were introduced, which made cigars faster and cheaper than workers could by hand. The impact of this invention was devastating for cigar makers. Puerto Ricans, particularly those that were black, had migrated to Tampa since the early years of the twentieth century (Greenbaum 1986: 16–20; Mormino and Pozzetta 1987).

Cigar-making firms located within the Southwark enclave, owned by Spanish-speakers, provided jobs for Latinos from the neighborhood. Between 1910 and 1945, no less than twenty-eight cigar making firms operated within the greater Spanish-speaking enclave areas of Southwark. Latinos owned all of these cigar-making firms. The largest tobacco-processing factory in the city at the time, the Bayuk Brothers Co,, employed many Spanish-speaking men and women. The Bayuk was located within walking distance of the Southwark enclave.

Changing Racial/Ethnic Panorama in Philadelphia

Puerto Rican migrants who arrived in Philadelphia during the first three decades of the twentieth century did so in the midst of growing racial and ethnic diversity of the city reflective of increased labor migration. Spanish-speakers, other European-born immigrants as well as African Americans made up the bulk of the new migrants in the city. African Americans began arriving from the South in large numbers during World War. I. Many had been recruited to work in war industries. Eastern and Southern European immigration especially from Poland, Italy, and Jews from Russia, contributed to the increase of the foreign born population in Philadelphia in this period (Mormino and Pozzetta 1987: 588).

The period between the Great Depression and the end of World War II (1929–1945) was marked by ebbs and flows but continued migration. Although there existed poor economic conditions both in Puerto Rico and in the U.S. during these years, the island's total dependence on the U.S. and the captive economy to American sugar and tobacco interests impacted the patterns of migration during this period.

During the first years of the Depression the flow of people from Puerto Rico to Philadelphia declined, momentarily. Although initially stunned by the impact of the Depression, notwithstanding, by the mid-1930s Puerto Ricans renewed migration to Philadelphia. Despite the hardships of the Depression era in Philadelphia, many Puerto Ricans believed that there were better opportunities in the city than there were back home on the island. The migratory trend to Philadelphia continued to increase through World War II. Between 1941 and 1945, more than 50,000 Puerto Ricans left the island for the United States; about 1,000 of those moved to Philadelphia.

During World War II, labor shortages in key industries and agriculture brought many Puerto Rican contracted laborers to the region. These laborers eventually moved to the city and joined those early pioneers who had preceded them and were already there to form a more visible presence.

In the early 1930s, Puerto Ricans who moved to Philadelphia found a city that, despite the brutal effects of the Depression still showed signs of vitality. Mayor Henry A. Mackey had asked for a study for the construction of a parkway between Race and Vine Streets from Broad to Delaware Avenue. The population of the city at the time was 1,950,000 representing a seven percent increase from 1920. Philadelphia was the third largest city in the country at the time. Native-born whites were the majority with 1,359,837, while there were 219,599 black and 368,624 foreign born. There was major construction going on in 1930 such as the addition of the 30th Street station.[14] The Mayor's Office issued (in English and in Spanish) "Philadelphia, Historic in the Past, Inviting in the Present, Superb in the Future", a promotional piece to boost business and tourism. In the 1930s, the city invested in more subways and rail lines rather than constructing highways like Los Angeles and Detroit. The Broad Street line had been extended north to South Street. Home ownership in Philadelphia in this period proved greater, with cheaper housing stock as compared to Boston and New York (Tincom 1982: 601, 608).

In 1941, Domingo Martinez arrived in Philadelphia with his wife Esther. Martinez, who was originally from the southern town of Salinas, near Ponce, Puerto Rico had first moved to New York City in 1936, where he had a brother residing. Possessing a keen business sense, Martinez initially went to work for a Spaniard who owned a grocery store in the busy sector along Marshall Street in the Northern Liberties section of the city. Martinez subsequently went into business with the owner and on weekends sold Spanish produce out of the trunk of his car along the streets where Puerto Ricans lived. Eventually Martinez and his wife took over ownership of the grocery store. His business later expanded to include the sale of airline tickets to and from Puerto Rico. Martinez became an important leader in the Puerto Rican community in Philadelphia, active in many civic affairs from the late 1940s through the 1970s. More Puerto Ricans followed the Martinezes to Philadelphia during World War II. The movement of Puerto Rican workers to the mainland, both under contract and on their own, was not a new phenomenon (Hernandez 1968).

The U.S. entry into World War II spurred the American economy. As in World War I, Philadelphia prepared again to be the "Arsenal of America". Fear of foreigners, especially the enemy, led the FBI to raid German and Italian organizations, social club and private homes during the war. To thwart repression similar to the ones that occurred during World War I, a rally was held by eleven different nationalities to express support for the war effort. The event took place on December 12, 1941, barely five days after Pearl Harbor. In addition, by the end of World War II a total of 182,850 Philadelphians were in the military service (Tincom 1982: 640).

On the industrial front, more than 3,500 businesses sold military supplies of all kinds. The Filch plant produced bombsights for radar. The famous Baldwin Locomotive Works produced guns, tanks, shell casings, armor plates, propellers and diesel engines in addition to the locomotives for which it was known. The E.G. Bud Company, which made trolleys before the war turned to the production of aircraft parts instead. The Disston Company made light armor instead of saws and other companies produced mosquito nets, ski equipment for mountain crews and parachute silk. Shipbuilding in Philadelphia grew incredibly during the war. No less than two hundred and fifty vessels were constructed between December 1941 and September 1945. By 1940, full employment in Philadelphia was a practical reality as most key industries operated at full capacity.

The United States entry into World War II also put enormous pressure on the country to mobilize labor and production to unprecedented levels. The millions of workers who left their jobs to enter the Armed Forces had to be replaced quickly. In 1942, President Franklin D. Roosevelt created the War Manpower Commission (WMC) to coordinate the efforts to secure sufficient workers to meet the demands of industry in the wartime economy. By 1943, many industries were desperately seeking workers, especially in the food production sector, and the WMC obliged by arranging the importation of foreign laborers to meet this need. To oversee regional needs, the WMC organized local offices to communicate their labor requirements with businesses assist in the contracting process. The shortage of manpower was more evident in the shipyards, prompting a request to import laborers.

Renewed migration to Philadelphia of blacks from the South could not by itself, fill the labor shortage. By 1943, the labor shortage was severe; the War Manpower Commission described the situation as critical and undertook drastic measures to address these conditions. Even German POWs were used in some industries. The Philadelphia Regional Office of the WMC was assigned the responsibility for Pennsylvania, New Jersey and Delaware. Specifically, the Joint Philadelphia-Camden Area Council was set up to address the pressing need for labor in both cities. [15]

Labor shortages in the United States compounded by the unemployment and material shortages on the island provided more than sufficient incentive for migration of Puerto Rican laborers to the States during the war. Also, the impact of the war on Puerto Rico underscored the island's dependency on the U.S. economy. There was a lack of sugarcane and citrus enterprises. Increased unemployment, social unrest and labor needs in the United States combined for the shipment of Puerto Rican workers (Giusti 1975: 8). Rexford Guy Tugwell, Puerto Rico's Governor from 1941–46 and an original member of Roosevelt's New Deal brain trust, implored Federal authorities to transport Puerto Rican workers to labor-hungry factories in the United States (Giusti 1975: 9).

The Philadelphia region had been acutely struck by labor shortages since as early as 1942. The Campbell Soup Company, in particular was one of the hardest pressed industries in the area.[16] To help Campbell and other area businesses, the WMC arranged to recruit laborers from the Caribbean including Jamaica, Trinidad and Puerto Rico.[17] One of those contracted in 1943 by the Campbell Soup was Marcelino Benitez, from the town of Carolina in Puerto Rico. He worked in Camden but lived in Philadelphia at fellow Puerto Rican, Antonio Malpica's boarding house located at 8th and Callowhill in the "tenderloin" section of Northern Liberties, home to most of the meatpacking plants in Philadelphia (Canales 1999).

Some time later, Juan Canales, prompted by letters from Benitez, came to work for the Campbell Soup Company. Canales, who was also from the same hometown as Benitez, arrived in Philadelphia via New York in the spring 1944. Once he contacted Benitez and secured employment at Campbell Soup, Canales also moved into Malpica's boarding house. Benitez, Malpica, Martinez and Rodriguez are all examples of networks formed to assist Puerto Ricans secure jobs and housing in Philadelphia during the war. These networks were consolidated and expanded after the war (Canales 1999).

Despite the initial satisfaction of, industries that hired Puerto Ricans workers, displeasure soon cropped up on both ends of the contract. On the one hand Campbell Soup and others could only hire Puerto Rican workers for 10–12 weeks a year, during critical time periods. Juan Canales, who worked for Campbell Soup during these few years tired of the seasonal nature of the job; he like many other Puerto Ricans found other employment. In 1947, after working for three years at Campbell Soup, Juan Canales became a merchant marine and spent the next thirty years traveling to different corners of the world (Canales 1999).

Puerto Rican contract laborers were supposed to return to the island once the job was done. This part of the contract proved very difficult to enforce because, as U.S. citizens, Puerto Ricans could not be deported. Many Puerto Ricans abandoned their jobs as contract laborers after short periods in the States, in some instances making allegations of mistreatment (*Business Week* 1944a: 10).[18] Puerto Rican workers complained of the awful conditions in which they were housed, the quality of the food they were served, and the lack of basic recreational facilities. [19] Consequently, many Puerto Rican workers at Campbell Soup and other wartime industries in the region sought employment in Philadelphia and formed part of the growing community in the city. Many responded to their Preacher, the Reverend Enrique Rodriguez and his Deacon, Domingo Martinez and joined other Spanish-speakers in the city and formed part of the welcome mat for the large influx of Puerto Rican migrants that arrived in Philadelphia after 1945.[20]

Conclusion

In Philadelphia, Puerto Ricans managed to connect with other Spanish-speakers, especially Spaniards, Cubans and Mexicans or other compatriots and secured housing and employment. On many occasions, Puerto Ricans not only shared neighborhoods with their Spanish-speaking neighbors but also with Polish, Italian, Jewish and black residents. These other labor migrants, especially Spanish-speakers, contributed as well to the diversity of Puerto Rican neighborhoods. For almost 100 years, small groups of Puerto Ricans progressively moved to and established residence in Philadelphia. Their political and economic struggles created the highway for others to follow. Once the Island became a U.S. colony and citizenship was imposed in 1917, the highway widened. This is the subject of the next chapter.

CHAPTER 3

Puerto Rican Settlement Patterns: Development of a Barrio

Introduction

In the early decades of the twentieth century Puerto Ricans in Philadelphia went from living dispersed throughout the City to encompass the formation and development of their respective settlements within the changing racial and ethnic composition of Philadelphia at that time. Puerto Rican migrants arriving in the City during those interwar years were impacted by the dramatic population shift as the growth of the African American community and the consolidation of white ethnic residents created racially segregated spaces in the city. I point out that the development of residential patterns among Puerto Ricans while interspersed within both white and black neighborhoods progressively led Puerto Ricans to share more common space with African Americans who were the most segregated group in the city. This chapter also reviews housing patterns in Philadelphia during the 1920s and 30s and the residential patterns of the Pan-Hispanic enclaves within them, patterns that influenced where many Puerto Rican migrants settled after 1945.

During the first years of the twentieth century, Philadelphia neighborhoods underwent significant changes as their ethnic and racial compositions and the City's landscape evolved with the influx of newer immigrants and migrants. Initially, Puerto Ricans in Philadelphia lived more dispersed than concentrated. By 1910, however, Puerto Ricans started to become more concentrated as the City of Neighborhoods became more segregated. As has already been discussed during the early decades of the twentieth century Latinos in the City began to concentrate in predominantly three neighborhoods: Spring Garden, Northern Liberties, North Philadelphia and in Southwark, neighborhoods they shared with a high concentration of Italian, Polish, Russian Jewish immigrants as well as with African Americans. Examples of the early Puerto Rican settlement patterns are exemplified by people like Saturnino Dones, who though originally settled in Southwark, close to the Bayuk Brothers Cigar factories, he subsequently moved to North Philadelphia where he lived close to the offices of the Cigar Makers International Union, Local # 165. He served for some time as an organizer for the CMIU, Dones spent most of his twenty years in Philadelphia living in North Philadelphia. In fact, Dones may have been one of the first Puerto Ricans in North Philadelphia. In 1910, he resided at 1121 Oakdale Street about 6 blocks away from where 50 years later Puerto Ricans would found the Taller Puertorriqueño, a major cultural organization located on N. 5th Street (U.S. Department of Commerce 1910).[1] He was 29 years old at the time and lived there with his wife, Bienvenida Barzilay, who was born in England of an English father and Dutch mother. The Dones had been married for two years and had a one-year old son, Daniel Thomas born in Philadelphia.

Antonio Malpica, who plied his trade of cigar making initially in South Philadelphia, later in Southwark, eventually settled in Northern Liberties where he opened up his own cigar making operation at 803 Callowhill Street. Another example was that of Jose DeCelis, who married and permanently settled in the Spring Garden area. For more than four decades, he resided at 862 N. 20th Street. Yet, another example was that of Tomas and Mary Rodriguez who first settled in Northern Liberties in 1931, shortly thereafter they moved to Spring Garden where Tomas was able to walk to his job as a drug tester at the Smith, Klein and French pharmaceutical company. The location of Puerto Rican settlements was centered in these three areas because of the inexpensive housing available at the time and the proximity to work available nearby. Over the course of the next four decades, housing in Philadelphia shifted by race and ethnicity. The impact of this shift contributed to the concentration of Puerto Ricans in neighborhoods that in the post-World War II period became segregated by race and ethnicity. The housing experience that Puerto Ricans confronted in this period shaped the future formation of this community and the long-term legacies for the post-1945 era that these earlier years bequeathed.[2]

Housing in the City of Neighborhoods

Despite the expansion of new housing in the outskirts of the city, the fact remained that most working-class families lacked adequate housing. Even with a home building boom in other parts of the city and surrounding suburbs, Philadelphia's slums continued to expand in the 1920's. Philadelphia's housing problems were well known. There was great speculation going on with the rate of rentals, throughout this period. Where there was new housing it was priced out of range for the common worker, with little provision of adequate dwellings. Clearly, Puerto Ricans, like many other Spanish-speakers who arrived in Philadelphia during World War I to work in war production industries, found the housing market extremely difficult. No matter where they lived in the period of the 1930s, Puerto Ricans and blacks generally resided in the oldest, most deplorable housing (Bausman 1987: 3, 10, 121; Varbero 1974: 84).

The housing experience that Puerto Ricans confronted in this period shaped the future formation of this community in the post-World War II period. In part, housing policies developed by both the federal and local governments, particularly those that were instituted during the Great Depression, eventually limited the housing stock available to Puerto Ricans. Housing policies during the first half of the twentieth century in Philadelphia led to major segregation and separation between the native white and the foreign-born white population, on the one hand, and African-American and Puerto Ricans on the other. Since Puerto Ricans and other Spanish-speakers were mostly working-class and poor, this was one characteristic they shared with Italians, Russian Jews, Poles and blacks. Consequently, their enclaves developed in the midst of working-class communities.

The dwellings were mostly three-story, generally with two apartments on each floor. These were row houses whose earlier history of the well to-do previous owners was evident by generous proportions and entrance foyer, almost always tiled. But, by the time Puerto Ricans and other Spanish-speakers began moving into these areas in substantial numbers, the deterioration of over-crowding and lack of maintenance began to set in. These conditions led to the relative bleakness of these dwellings and they became little more than shells for the protection from the weather at times with four, six or even eight families sharing the space. To add further to the deterioration and over-use of these dwellings, many were sub-divided into small two- to four-room apartments, with as many as twenty people to an apartment (Koss 1965: 80–1).

Between 1890 and the beginning of World War I, Philadelphia underwent major housing construction. It was however, the areas outside of the old-Penn Grid that saw the expansion of housing during the first decades of the twentieth century. Several miles of two and three story single-family row houses were built "along the outer edges of the city." The First World War had an enormous impact on Philadelphia's housing situation. The need for wartime workers increased the city's population by more than 200,000 people. At the same time, home building in the city decreased from 7,762 units in 1916 to 965 in 1918 (Hardy 1989: 131).

Philadelphia in the early twentieth century did not suffer the same high concentration of tenement housing as did such cities as New York and Chicago. However, the city did have serious housing problems. Even though Philadelphia did not have an overwhelming number of tenements, generally defined as having three or more families, the worst housing of the city in the first decades of the twentieth century was in tenements and in scattered alleys. Of the two types of houses, the tenement dwellers were worse off than those that lived in alley houses. In one case in particular, serious overcrowding was found when 65 tenements were inspected by city officials in 1905 and in one block alone found that 55 of them "made no pretense of complying with the law requiring fire escapes". The inspection revealed serious overcrowding with families sharing up to three rooms with more than a dozen lodgers. In 1914, a housing study conducted on tenement owners in Philadelphia charged with violations indicated, that 105 properties were located in the Second, Third and Fifth wards, the heart of the Italian, Russian and Spanish-speaking enclaves in Southwark (Klein 1980: 348–9; Sutherland 1976: 189).

The type of housing that most Puerto Ricans occupied in the Spring Garden and Northern Liberties sections of the city differed somewhat from Southwark. In those two areas the transformation that occurred with the housing stock resembled more the transition of the affluent moving out than that in Southwark. Three story dwellings, many of which had been in the hands of the wealthy, especially, charac- terized Spring Garden. When the owners began to leave prior to World War I, many of these dwellings were quickly converted into multi-apartment buildings to meet the growing demand of an increased workforce that labored in wartime industries. Similarly, parts of Northern Liberties' housing were also transformed. The story in Southwark was somewhat different in that, not only was the housing stock trans- formed to accommodate more newcomers, but also the housing stock in this part of the city was among the oldest at the time. Some houses in Southwark were already one hundred years old at the beginning of World War I. None of these three areas saw any of the new housing construction that occurred in the city during the first two decades before World War I.

During the war years housing construction came almost to a complete standstill. Military priorities laid claim to key supplies like lumber, steel and other materials indispensable for housing construction. The housing shortage for black workers had been evident since World War I. Black workers in wartime industries in Philadel- phia had been relegated to "colored sections." Consequently, this contributed to over- crowding. Though the Philadelphia Housing Association succeeded in persuading realtors to rent to blacks in white occupied areas, especially those that were close to wartime plants and industries, some racial strife ensured (Franklin 1979: 26).

Areas of Northern Liberties and Southwark were especially affected by the se- vere housing situation where a furnished room district developed. Formed by the Sixth, Tenth, Eleventh, Twelfth, Thirteenth and Fourteenth wards, the area was bound- ed by Chestnut Street on the south, and Poplar street in the north, the Delaware river on the east and Broad street on the west. In addition to the difficulties of a lack of new housing, these areas also saw the development of rooming houses. In South- wark, three-fourths of the houses not occupied by immigrants had been converted to furnished rooms. The merchant class of the neighborhood formally occupied these homes. The homes were large, three-story structures with two parlors, a dining room and a kitchen or two on the first floor. On the second floor was a large bedroom in the front, a smaller bedroom, a bath and a study room. On the third floor there were two to four box bedrooms (Fretz 1911: 6, 10–1).

By 1920, the city's housing shortage had reached dramatic proportions. At the beginning of the second decade of the twentieth century, it was estimated that the city's housing shortage was well over 20,000. Even though homebuilders began construction on 12,000 new units in 1922, it failed to meet the city's 30,000 annual increase in the population. Also, the Philadelphia Housing Association contributed more than 20 percent of the housing construction and conversions between 1921 and 1923. Yet, as PHA Executive Secretary at the time, Bernard Newman pointed out, many speculators converted dwellings at a faster rate than city inspectors could check for building code violations. This practice led to many unsafe living quarters for the city's poor and newly arriving immigrants. In particular, public housing was supposed to be the opposite: provide better housing for the industrial working class. At least that is what late nineteenth and early twentieth century reformers believed. Not only was public housing to provide employment to idle construction workers, but also hope for a more humane social order (Bausman 1987: xii, 12; Jackson 1987).

In the 1920's, Philadelphia reigned as an industrial city with a large concentration of textile and metal manufacturing. On the other hand, though, the city's huge housing stock of two and three story brick row homes was woefully unsafe. These small tenements, situated just north and south of downtown were mostly dark back alleys and courts in Southwark, Poplar and Northern Liberties that lacked modern heating and plumbing; beyond those courts and alleyways stood a much sturdier ring of row houses. These homes had been built during an earlier housing boom between 1850 and 1900. By 1920, these older sections of the city counted over 200,000 housing units that were built in the nineteenth century. The residents of these homes were primarily low-income workers (Bausman 1987: 3; Varbero 1974: 86).

South Philadelphia also contained the oldest and most obsolete school buildings in the city during the 1920s. Wards one through four, twenty-six, thirty-six, thirty-nine and forty-eight had the oldest buildings in the city. Generally speaking, the quality of life in the areas of Philadelphia in which Spanish speakers resided in this period was not very healthy. Judging from the housing conditions, particularly in Southwark, most migrants did all they could to adapt given the poor living conditions and availability. Many single men opted to live in cheap lodging. More than a few Spanish-speaking families also opted to turn their homes into lodgings, especially for single men (Varbero 1974: 246).

From Dispersed Settlement to Ethnic Enclaves

The years between the Civil War and the Great Depression marked a significant alteration in residential segregation in Philadelphia denoted by income and ethnicity. This is key in understanding the development of the Puerto Rican community in the city. The previous clustering of skilled workers into ethnic communities began to shift in the early decades of the twentieth century as more of them, able to buy homes, began to spread out around the city, whereas the unskilled workers continued to live in poorer neighborhoods. Many unskilled immigrant workers lived in some of the most ethnically \concentrated communities like Southwark and Spring Garden. This was also true for Puerto Ricans and other Latinos (Warner 1987: 8).

As indicated above, the Puerto Rican settlement in Philadelphia was initially dispersed but it became more concentrated after World War I. This concentration was due to the influx of wartime workers and the establishment of community institutions. Puerto Ricans settled in areas in which Spaniards, Cubans and Mexicans were the premier Latino groups. These areas developed around work and church. Pan-Hispanic enclaves like those that evolved in Southwark, Spring Garden and Northern Liberties contained the bulk of Puerto Rican residents in Philadelphia in the years between 1910 and 1945.[3]

Between 1910 and 1930, Puerto Rican settlement patterns shifted from widespread dispersal to concentration. Puerto Ricans also tended to live near each other rather than be spread out throughout neighborhoods. An analysis of the location of persons with Spanish-surnames who were residents of the city between 1910 and 1930 provides a glimpse into their settlement patterns. Although Puerto Ricans lived in many sections of the city, more than eighty-five percent of this sample were concentrated in the sections closest to Center City. For 1910, using a sample of approximately two hundred Spanish surnamed individuals residing in Philadelphia at the time, indicates that Hispanics were concentrated in sections of South and Southwest Philadelphia, North Philadelphia and West Philadelphia closest to Center City. The south and southwest settlements were concentrated in Southwark and Grays Ferry, respectively. Although both sections were heavily white ethnic (Italians and Polish), these neighborhoods also included a large concentration of African-Americans as well (see maps).

The most striking aspect of Puerto Rican and other Spanish-speaking residential distribution in Philadelphia between 1910 and 1930, however, was not intense segregation, but rather the widespread dispersal through certain areas in central and North Philadelphia. Instead of being tightly clustered residentially, Puerto Ricans would remain a settlement of scattered enclaves until the major demographic changes that occurred in the late 30s and 40s, when a cohesive Puerto Rican barrio emerged.

Map 1. The three neighborhoods (circled) reflect where the bulk of Puerto Ricans resided during the 1910–1945 period. After WW II, Puerto Ricans began pushing further into North Philadelphia.

The earliest Puerto Rican settlements depended on the availability of work, and the formation of subsequent colonias depended on the accessibility to cheap housing, good transportation and shopping. Considering these demands, the movement of Puerto Ricans into certain geographic areas and the conversion of them into distinct enclaves increased during the late twenties and thirties. In forming these enclaves, many Spanish-speakers, particularly Puerto Ricans, attempted to recreate network patterns common to their native villages or towns back home. These areas contained some of the city's oldest housing stock along with cramped alleyways. This northernmost section of South Philadelphia, called Southwark, had developed early as a classic American working class district. This was the area in which many immigrants became acquainted with life in industrial America, Philadelphia (Warner 1987: 9).[4] (See maps.)

Puerto Ricans and other Latinos also established other enclaves in the southeastern portions of North Philadelphia, which was predominantly African-American and Jewish. Others concentrated in the northwestern section of North Philadelphia, which was mostly Italian, or in west Kensington which was mostly Hungarian and Jewish. These areas along with the older, more established enclaves in Southwark, Spring Garden and Northern Liberties, housed the bulk of the Puerto Rican population in Philadelphia in the years before the Second World War (Santiago 1994).

Most Spanish-speaking residents though remained in the areas of Southwark, Spring Garden and Northern Liberties. One of the difficulties in calculating precise numbers of Puerto Ricans and other Spanish-speakers in Philadelphia for the first half of the twentieth century is that the Census Bureau, in that period, was not consistent in categorizing Spanish-surname residents. As U.S. citizens, Puerto Ricans did not always figure in immigrant counts. In 1910, for instance, the U.S. Census Bureau counted Spaniards and Puerto Ricans as a separate group while Cubans and other Spanish-speaking groups were not counted that way. The 1910 census, by the way, was the first to officially count Puerto Ricans in the U.S. as a separate ethnic group. In the 1920 census, Cubans and Puerto Ricans were counted but not Spaniards or other groups. Mexicans, who were counted as a separate group in the 1900 census, were not included as a separate group again until the 1930 census. However, with more recent access to manuscript census data now available on-line it is possible to substantially reconstruct the histories of these important enclaves.[5]

The largest concentration of Pan-Hispanics in this interwar period was in an enclave located within the neighborhood of Southwark. The enclave was bounded by Fifth Street on the west, Locust Street on the north, Second Street on the east and Bainbridge Street on the south. The northern section of this enclave known as Society Hill, had once been the home to old Philadelphia's rich families and well to-do German Jews, but by the First World War many of these areas had become more working-class ethnic enclaves. In this time period Puerto Ricans and other Spanish-speakers shared the area mostly with representations of the "new" immigrants of the time: the Polish and the Italians (Whiteman 1976: 241)—see maps.

Southwark

The enclave of Southwark was centered along the market known as the Head House that ran north and south along Second Street between Pine and South streets.[6] According to a report prepared for the International Institute in the early 1920s, the broader boundaries of the concentration of Latinos in the Southwark enclave included Pine and Bainbridge Streets on the north and south and the Delaware River and 5th Street on the east and west. The report also confirmed the scattered nature of Spanish-speaking residents in Philadelphia by referring to pockets of Hispanics further south in the city, as well as in Kensington and West Philadelphia. Significant in this report was the allusion to the existence of a community that included a professional class; businesses and mutual help groups as well. The report also highlighted that Spaniards were the predominant group of Hispanics in this area. Cigar manufacturing in Philadelphia in the early decades of the twentieth century was concentrated in the areas of west Southwark, Northern Liberties and North Philadelphia. It is no wonder that many Puerto Rican cigar makers in this time period also resided in these same neighborhoods. The largest cigar manufacturing company in the city at the time: the Bayuk Brothers Cigar Company, Inc., which employed many Spanish-speaking men and women, was located on the southwest corner of Bainbridge and 10th Streets in the heart of Southwark.[7]

The 1923 study by Fermina Martinez found 10 major cigar making firms owned by either Spaniards or Cubans in Philadelphia at the time. Several like Jose Alvarez located a 58 S. 2nd Street, Juan G. Blanco located at 42 N. 11 Street, Charles Lasa located at 1343 Arch Street, Ramon Azoque & Co, located at 808 Chestnut and Bienvenido G. Padilla located at 103 N. 5th Street were situated in or around the Southwark settlements. The others: Montero Cigars Mfg. Co, located at 1610 Susquehanna Avenue, Isidor M. Hernandez located at 1543 Susquehanna, Caballero located 1824 Ridge Avenue, where Martinez found many Hispanic women working and Frank Estrada located at 3242 W. Allegheny Avenue, where Saturnino Dones worked for a while, were all found in North Philadelphia.[8]

Spring Garden

By 1910, a clear picture of the residential patterns of Puerto Ricans in Spring Garden began to emerge. The enclave, though concentrated in certain blocks, was more spread out than the one in Southwark, thereby covering a larger geographic area. The concentration of Spanish-speakers was in the northeast quadrant of the Fifteenth ward. In this area, Puerto Ricans shared the neighborhood with "older" immigrant groups, especially the Irish. The area also had a very large concentration of Polish immigrants along with some Italians (U.S. Department of Commerce 1910).[9]

A review of the 1910 manuscript census indicates that Puerto Ricans in Spring Garden were concentrated in an area bounded by 18th Street on the west, Girard Avenue on the north, Broad Street on the east, and Vine Street on the south. The Latino group in Spring Garden was diverse, besides Puerto Ricans, the enclave also included Spaniards, Cubans, Mexicans, Hondurans, Salvadorans, Chileans and Peruvians. In addition, there were Hispanics that had inter-married with native-born whites. The Spanish-speaking households in this census did not appear to be as overcrowded as those in Southwark but numbers of them included a high degree of boarders living in the same household. Most migrants in this sector had arrived to the United States before the turn of the century, some as early as 1880. The few recent arrivals had done so between 1904 and 1908 (U.S. Department of Commerce 1910).

By 1920, the Spring Garden enclave reflected the growth of the Spanish-speaking population in the city. Many of these residents that were counted in this census had arrived during World War I. In 1920, DeCelis, who had graduated from Temple in 1918, was living at 862 N. 20th Street. He would remain there until the end of WW II. He lived there with his wife Martha, an American of Irish descent, their nine-month old daughter Martha and his wife's grandparents Charles A. and Martha Sawyer. In addition, DeCelis' had a boarder, a medical student named Juan Del Rio who had arrived from Puerto Rico in 1916 (U.S. Department of Commerce 1920: Enumeration District 306 16A; *Boyd's Philadelphia City Directory* 1919–1920).[10]

The 1920 census also recorded an even more concentrated enclave in Spring Garden, indicated by, among other things, an expansion in the number of boarding houses catering to Spanish-surnamed men (U.S. Department of Commerce 1920).[11] The housing stock in this neighborhood, especially along Spring Garden, Mount Vernon, Green and Wallace streets were three or four stories high. They were originally built for wealthy families who left in the early 20th century for the communities developed in the West Philadelphia vicinity. These structures were ideal for subdivision. One example of this was the home of Sebastian R. Romagosa located at 1636 Green Street. Romagosa, a Cuban dentist, lived at this location with his wife Jeannette and son Samuel. He also housed no less than 14 male boarders. Four of Romagosa boarders: Rafael Camacho, the Rivera brothers: Ramon and Angel and Emanuel Barbosa were Puerto Ricans the others were Cubans and Mexicans. All of the boarders were machinists who worked at the Baldwin Locomotives Works Company located on Broad and Spring Garden Streets had also arrived in the U.S. during WW I. Romagosa worked at his own office while his wife managed the boarding house (U.S. Department of Commerce 1920: Population, Enumerator Districts #s 293 10 B). In the 1920s, this area represented one of the fastest growing in the city. Spring Garden was characterized by a modest amount of ethnic and racial residential occupancy (U.S. Department of Commerce 1920: Population). There was also an increase in the establishment of lodging for single women, many of them recent arrivals. Eighty-five percent of the Spanish-speaking residents of Spring Garden in 1920 had arrived in the United States between 1914–1919, with 65 percent having arrived between 1917 and 1919 (U.S. Department of Commerce 1920: Population).

Northern Liberties
A third concentration of Puerto Ricans during the first decades of the twentieth century was located in the Northern Liberties area. Historically, Northern Liberties had existed since the time of the American Revolution when its land value had received high assessments by the local government. After the Revolution, when a serious housing problem developed in Philadelphia, Northern Liberties was identified as an ideal place for development, and land there was auctioned off to alleviate the situation. Northern Liberties quickly became a bustling residential area. By the time of the Civil War, the upper section of Northern Liberties already constituted an important working-class district and was a haven for many ex-slaves who gathered there in large numbers (Blumin 1976: 39, 43; Sutherland 1976: 175; Hershberg 1976: 122).

In Northern Liberties, the Pan-Hispanic enclave was divided into two sections: the area south of Spring Garden Street where the meatpacking plants were located and commonly referred to as the *tenderloin*. The second section located north of Spring Garden Street was called "Marshall Street". The Hispanic sections of the tenderloin in Northern Liberties had been clearly identified since the 1920s. The largest Spanish-speaking sector of the *tenderloin* was bordered by Spring Garden Street on the north, Seventh Street on the east, Vine Street on the south and 10th Street on the west. A second, smaller section of Hispanics was located in the area bordered by Spring Garden Street on the north, 3rd Street on the east, Noble Street on the north and Orianna Street on the south. This area also included burlesque theaters, cabarets, dance halls, prostitution and gambling houses.[12]

In the mid- 1930s, Antonio Malpica moved from the Southwark enclave into the Puerto Rican enclave in the heart of the tenderloin section of Northern Liberties. He rented a building located at 803 Callowhill near 8th Street and lived there until his death in 1952. Malpica had learned his cigar making craft in Puerto Rico. Before

moving to Philadelphia he had lived in Old San Juan Puerto Rico at #86 San Sebastian street and worked at a nearby cigar factory (U.S. Department of Commerce 1910:
Population—Puerto Rico, Enumeration District No. 2, Sheet No. 29). Although he
first settled at 1704 Wallace Street in Spring Garden with his wife Mercedes and his
son Abelardo soon thereafter moved to Northern Liberties. At the location on Callowhill Street, Malpica converted the first floor into a storefront cigar shop he called
"Malpica's Havana Cigars." According to his son Jesse, Malpica not only made hand-
made cigars that he sold to patrons of his shop by the box-loads, but also produced
cigars for a cigar factory located in the Marshall street area of Northern Liberties.[13]

Malpica was not only an entrepreneur cigar maker; he also managed the dwell-
ing at 803 Callowhill Street as a boarding house for single men. Malpica's place
housed mostly Puerto Rican men, many of whom worked for the Campbell Soup
Company in Camden, New Jersey. During World War II the number of Puerto Rican
laborers at Campbell increased and at least two of those workers, Marcelo Benitez'
and Juan Canales, lived at Malpica's boarding house during that time. It is unclear
just how Benitez learned about Malpica's place, but Canales learned about it from
his hometown friend Benitez. Juan Canales arrived in Philadelphia in the spring of
1944, went to work at the Campbell Soup Company and resided at Malpica's place. In
addition to Benitez and Canales, Malpica's other boarders also included a number of
Spanish-speaking merchant marines that worked for shipping companies in Philadelphia (Bermudez 1999; Canales 1999).

Malpica's boarders shopped for food and clothing at the Marshall Street market that ran north and south between Spring Garden Street and Girard Avenue in
the northern section of Northern Liberties. This street market characterized the
northern section, which was very similar to the Italian Market that ran along 9th
Street in South Philadelphia. This area of Northern Liberties was bordered by
Spring Garden Street on the south and Girard Avenue in the North, but also 10th
street on the west and Front street on the east. Jewish merchants owned most of
the pushcarts and storefronts along Marshall Street but little by little, Spanish-
speakers also began to work there as well. The market was an important source of
employment and food supplier to Puerto Ricans Northern Liberties. In this area
Cubans, especially cigar makers and small shop owners along Marshall Street,
were the premier group.

Northern Liberties was once a well to-do Jewish area typified by Franklin Street.
This street built up by attractive limestone and brick houses was by the 1920s filled
with Eastern European Jewish immigrants as the earlier German-Jewish Immigrants, who became more affluent and *americanized,* moved out. Many of the earlier

Jewish immigrants, especially those from Western Europe looked upon the Jewish newer immigrants, particularly the poor from Russia with disdain. It was at this time that German Jews left Northern Liberties for other sections of the city like Logan, Hunting Park or the Northeast. Although many of the early Jewish groups left, those who remained did so because they preferred the convenience of the established Jewish businesses that ran along on Marshall Street (Whiteman 1976: 248–9). It was with this latter group of Jewish residents and businesses that Puerto Ricans, like Domingo Martinez, the entrepreneur encountered when they began occupying this sector in the 1930s and 1940s. Martinez became one of the first Puerto Rican businessmen in the Marshall Street area to open up a *bodega*.[14]

When the Bayuk Brothers Cigar Company moved from their location in Southwark, to 9th Street and Columbia Avenue in North Philadelphia, many cigar makers also moved closer to this location, especially to the northernmost sector of Marshall Street. This move contributed to the expansion of the Latino Northern Liberties enclave and created a corridor of housing, business, employment, and shopping opportunities for Puerto Ricans in the neighborhood. This area eventually became the southern section of the Puerto Rican community that evolved in the post-World War II period (Bermudez 1999).

The three enclave neighborhoods of Southwark, Spring Garden and Northern Liberties that Puerto Rican residents established during the first half of the twentieth century reflected, from a geographical perspective, larger overriding housing patterns developing in the city at that time. By this time period the city had already begun to exhibit segregated residential patterns. Some of these patterns continued fairly unabated into the second half of the twentieth-century. An analysis of the population shifts in Philadelphia between 1910 and 1940 provides evidence that suggest how residential patterns across the city developed and what impact it had on how and where Puerto Ricans selected neighborhoods in which to reside.

Shift in Residential Patterns in Philadelphia

During the first decades of the twentieth century, residential patterns in Philadelphia shifted dramatically. As in many other metropolitan cities, the development of new modes of transportation such as elevated trains and subways sped up the exodus toward the outer rims of the city. This factor contributed to a sorting out of the urban population by racial, ethnic or socio-economic groups and African-Americans were particularly affected by this segregation. In this period, Puerto Ricans developed residential patterns in Philadelphia that resembled more closely the experience of blacks than those of whites (native and foreign-born).

During this time, native-born whites began to move out from some of the older communities around the center of the city to the newly developed outer rims or the expanding suburbs. Increasingly, larger numbers of foreign-born whites also began to move out
of some of their former ethnic enclaves as well. Meantime, blacks, many of which had
begun arriving in Philadelphia in significant numbers during World War I, substituted
outgoing whites in the areas of Philadelphia which they vacated. Puerto Ricans and other
Latinos, many of whom like blacks, also arrived in larger numbers during World War I,
also came to occupy residences emptied out by whites (Kusmer 1976: 36).

The Puerto Rican and other Spanish-speaking groups in Philadelphia grew from
approximately 2,529 in 1910 to 6,854 by 1930. Also, the developing rigidity along racial
lines contributed to their solidarity as a group as they navigated and negotiated their
way through racial segregation evolving in the city at the time. This increase, although
evident in almost all wards of the city, was most significant in South Philadelphia, specifically in Southwark/Society Hill including the Fourth, Fifth and Sixth wards and the
Thirty-six and Twenty-eighth wards of Grays Ferry. There was also a marked increase
in Spring Garden's Fifteenth ward; and in the Thirty-second, Thirty-eighth and Forty-
third wards of North Philadelphia. The third area of significant increase was in the
West Philadelphia wards: The Twenty-fourth, twenty-seventh and Forty-fourth wards
of Parkside and Wynnefield and the Forty-six and Fortieth wards in Cobbs Creek.

In every section of Philadelphia in which Puerto Ricans lived, they shared the
neighborhoods with other ethnic groups. By 1930, when native-born and foreign-born
whites moved out of these communities in significant numbers seeking to ensure a better housing choice, Southwark and Spring Garden solidified their importance as areas
for newer migrants. Three of these groups, Eastern European Jews, Italians and Poles
the new immigrants, shared similar neighborhoods with Spanish-speakers in this period. However, as foreign-born white groups, they too followed the path of other white
groups in the other areas of the city. Italians eventually settled in a solid block in South
Philadelphia and Jews and Poles in North Philadelphia (Cutler and Gillete 1980).

In Southwark, Puerto Ricans crowded into small tenements along Lombard
Street between Second and Front streets, just off the Head House Market. The 1920
manuscript census enumeration districts for this area indicate severe overcrowding for Pan-Hispanic residencies. In addition, most homes in this area also included
the practice of the taking in of boarders. The same situation holds true for Spanish-
speaking residencies just south of this area along Second Street in the Sixth ward.
The Enumeration Districts from the census for these areas in the Fifth and Sixth
wards around Front and Second Streets south of Lombard Street also indicate a high
degree of boarders in Spanish-speaking households. In several Spanish-speaking

households surveyed over a spread of seven different wards, as indicated by the 1920 manuscript census, out of 82 individuals, (excluding spouses and children) who were listed as boarders (56) outnumbered renters (26) 2–1. In addition, there were only two homeowners in the whole group. One possible explanation for the high degree of boarders could be the time of arrival of these migrants. Fifty-two percent of the adults in this sample (53) had arrived in the United States between 1915 and 1920. Most of the recent arrivals were still employed in what had been wartime industries (U.S. Department of Commerce 1920).[15]

Housing during the Great Depression

The worst housing conditions in Philadelphia in 1936 were in the Center City slums, where over one third of the 93,000 residents were black. This area was also home to more than a third of Spanish-speakers who lived in the city at the time. One of the main settlements of this sector was Southwark. Fifth Street on the east, South Street on the south, the Schuylkill River on the west, and Spruce Street on the north bound this area, which Latinos shared with blacks (Bausman 1987: 32; Franklin 1979: 3).

Federal housing policies during the Depression also contributed to further residential segregation in Philadelphia and set the tone for the expansion of suburbs in the post-World War II period. This was evident nationwide, and in Philadelphia these policies contributed to further clustering of blacks, Puerto Ricans and poor people generally into certain areas of the city, areas that became the black and Spanish-speaking ghettos of notoriety during of the 1960s and beyond. The policies and practices of the Housing and Home Finance Agency and its constituent bodies, the Public Housing Administration (PHA), the Federal Housing Administration (FHA), and the Urban Renewal Administration (URA) all contributed to residential isolation of blacks in the country's major cities. In some instances, like New York, New Jersey and Philadelphia, Puerto Ricans were also channeled into and affected by these policies. PHA in particular was found to have contributed significantly to racial segregation by allowing local authorities to implement their respective housing policies according to their local mores, i.e. racial separation in the South and exclusive sight control and tenant selection practices in other parts of the country.

In a similar fashion, FHA's mortgage policies in this period were also shaped by racial segregation. Many blacks were excluded from home loans further isolating them in major cities. One policy that particularly affected Puerto Ricans living in Southwark and Spring Garden was what Arnold Hirsch called the "Negro clearance" programs of the URA. Some of the slum clearance programs begun in Philadelphia during the Depression and which were continued in the post-World War II period targeted areas of the city in which blacks and Puerto Ricans resided. Reformers viewed these areas, generally closest to the Center City, as important in the rejuvenation of the city. This practice pushed Puerto Ricans and blacks further into ghettos and effectively separated them from the Center City development (Hirsh 2000: 158–9).

In addition, some of the federal housing agencies including the Home Owners Loan Corporation and the FHA also implemented a residential appraisal system, which actually "redlined" certain communities where banks refused to give loans to blacks, Puerto Ricans and many other poor people. In the private sector, insurance companies like Prudential also got into the act of exclusionary housing policies following the federal climate established in the 1930s. The Depression had a tremendous impact on insurance companies who, up to that point had been largely involved in the business of providing housing mortgages. With the federal government's intrusion into housing through the FHA in 1934, insurance companies like Prudential of New Jersey shifted their investments to the purchase of government bonds. Since federal home loans were backed by the government, Prudential and other insurance companies jumped on the bandwagon and began to get into the housing market. Local exclusionary practices of these private companies resulted in few if any, black families benefiting from Prudential's lending policies.

Policies like those of Prudential and the FHA agencies focused on the suburban housing market and generally neglected the urban market. The suburban market was almost entirely white, and it was they who benefited from lending policies and mortgages for new homes in the suburbs at the cost of inner city housing markets, one that became progressively more black and Puerto Rican: poor and working-class. Thus, the displacement of black and Puerto Rican populations that occurred in Philadelphia in the 1950s actually had their birth in the federal government's housing policies implemented locally with total disregard for fairness and equity to minority racial and ethnic groups (Mohl 1998: 67; Rome 1994: 411; Hanchett 2000: 312–4).

Conclusion

Throughout the first half of the twentieth century, Philadelphia's population shifted dramatically. Racially and ethnically, the "City of Neighborhoods" became more segregated. As development of the outer rims of the city expanded, native-born whites moved out followed by foreign-born whites. Blacks occupied the neighborhoods and housing abandoned by whites and Puerto Ricans and other Latinos also moved into these areas as well. The housing stock in these communities, especially in Southwark and Northern Liberties where Spanish-speakers concentrated were the oldest and had the worst conditions. Federal and local housing policies contributed to this concentration. Puerto Ricans in the city in this time period were thus concentrated in the most racially and ethnically poorest and working-class areas of the city.

Puerto Rican migration to Philadelphia accelerated during the interwar period; it occurred at a time when the city's population shifted and housing policies made the city one of the most racially segregated cities in the North by the end of the twentieth century. These population and housing shifts had a tremendous impact on the Puerto Rican migrants and established long-term residential patterns that influenced where Puerto Ricans, who arrived in the post-World War II period came to live. The shift in population, the move of native-born whites to the suburbs and outer rims of the city, and the substitution of the outbound groups by new immigrants, including Puerto Ricans, contributed to the concentration of Latino enclaves in the city. Local and federal housing policies further restricted these newer migrants, especially African Americans and Puerto Ricans to specific neighborhoods in Philadelphia.

The population and economic activity that began to shift toward the suburbs in the 1920s accelerated after World War II. The shift to the suburbs also implied a shift in the industrial base of the city, a preview of the dramatic changes in job opportunities in the 1960s and 1970s. The next chapter explores job opportunities of Puerto Rican labor migrants in the interwar period and the implications for their future residential patterns and community development (Adams et al. 1991: 17, chapter 4).

Image 1. Baldwin Locomotive Works, Broad & Spring Garden Streets, early 20th century. Many Puerto Ricans worked there during WW I.
(Source: Campbell Collection, Historical Society of Pennsylvania)

Image 2. La Milagrosa Church, 1903
Spring Garden Street, Feb. 1915.
(Source: Boletin Mensual Publicado por
los Padres Misioneros de S. Vicente de
Paul, Historical Society of Pennsylvania)

Image 3. Bayuk Brothers Cigar Co distribution trucks, 1933.
(Source: Historical Society of Pennsylvania)

Image 4. Antonio Malpica, Philadelphia, ca. 1930.
(Source: Jesse Bermudez-Malpica)

*Image 5. First Communion, La Milagrosa's Spanish Catholic Club,
Brandywine Street, May, 1933.*

*Image 6. Tomas & Mary
Rodriguez and children, 1940s.*
(Source: Emma Rodriguez)

Image 7. Tomas Rodriguez,
Atlantic City, New Jersey, 1940s.
(Source: Emma Rodriguez)

Image 8. Marshall Street Markets near Girard Ave., 1940.
(Source: Philadelphia Record Photography Collection,
Historical Society of Pennsylvania)

Image 9. Fourth Annual Communion Breakfast, La Milagrosa, June 1950, Mary Rodriguez [Flowery dress] is seated front row, fourth from the right. Her daughters are seated on each side of her. (Source: Emma Rodriguez)

Image 10. Juan Canales, Philadelphia, 1945.
(Source: Zoraida Figueroa)

Image 11. Dr. Jose DeCelis, 1958.
(Philadelphia Evening Bulletin)

Image 12. Domingo Martinez, 1971.
(Philadelphia Evening Bulletin)

Image 13. Juan Canales & his wife,
Maria Julia, 1970s.
(Source: Zoraida Figueroa)

CHAPTER 4

Race, Class and Ethnicity: Puerto Rican's Employment Patterns

Introduction

In the previous chapters we examined the process of Puerto Rican migration to Philadelphia during the first half of the twentieth century. In addition, we saw how Puerto Ricans settled in multi ethnic communities. This chapter explores the job market Puerto Ricans found upon their arrival in Philadelphia, with a special emphasis on the interwar period and how labor segmentation, at the time, contributed to limiting future employment options for Puerto Ricans. Also, the issue of language probably served to limit the labor participation of many Puerto Ricans in Philadelphia. If the worker spoke only Spanish, this probably limited his or her opportunity in the Philadelphia labor market. The lack of skills transferable to U.S. labor markets was also an impediment to Puerto Ricans' occupational participation in Philadelphia.

At the beginning of the twentieth century, the Philadelphia economy was remarkably diverse. Before the turn of the century, 40 percent of the working population had been in clothing and textile manufacturing. The other 60 percent of Philadelphia workers were scattered across a wide range of industries, including: machine tools and hardware, shoes and boots, paper and printing, iron and steel, chemicals as well as shipbuilding. The largest industries in the city in 1900 were textiles and apparels. These two industries were made up mainly of small establishments. These small companies were relatively smaller than those of other similar mill towns like the ones in Lowell, Massachusetts, for instance. The distinction of smaller but diverse helped sustain a broad industrial base, a diversity that, in time may have spelled Philadelphia's early demise as an industrial center. Notwithstanding, in the early twentieth century Philadelphia offered a great variety of employment possibilities for migrants like Puerto Ricans and, in times of war, the city was an even greater occupational haven with many industries offering jobs in defense production (Adams et al. 1991: 6–8).

The city's structural limitations were particular to the industrial base which was made up largely of proprietorial ownership. During the first three decades of the twentieth century Philadelphia textiles, as Historian Phillip Scranton has pointed out, became a "sick" industry. This was a clear sign that a process of de-industrialization was beginning to take place in the city. It was no wonder that these particular industries felt greater effects of the Great Depression, especially those in the fashion industry. Although World War II breathed some life into Philadelphia's archaic industrial base, the positive economic effects on the city lasted just beyond the war years. Even though the city's textile industry continued to thrive until the 1950s, based on the wartime boost, the dye had been cast. In the midst of these economic and structural realities, Puerto Ricans and other Spanish-speakers arrived in Philadelphia worked, formed and developed their respective working-class enclaves amidst this reality and were affected by it (Scranton 1989: 9; Licht 1992: 11, 14).

Puerto Ricans who migrated to Philadelphia during the first half of the twentieth century were mostly working-class, though there were also a number of professionals and businessmen as well. Initially semi-skilled workers, like cigar makers and others, were more representative of these migrants. Progressively, however, from the 1920s through the 1940s, more diverse laborers from the island joined in the migration process to Philadelphia. Possessing fewer industrial skills, many Puerto Ricans joined other "new" immigrant workers as well as African American migrants who came up from the South to the City of Brotherly Love.

Among the Puerto Ricans who came in the early years, many of them had been members of the Federación Libre de Trabajadores (FLT) [the Free Workers Federation] in Puerto Rico, the island's premier labor organization. This labor connection did not offer them any special edge in the United States, however, since many of these workers found themselves essentially excluded from labor unions with some exceptions like the Cigar Makers International Union (CMIU). The occupational trend of Puerto Ricans in the period between 1910 and 1930 was largely one of decline in status, a decline which accelerated in the 1930s and 1940s. This decline can be gleaned from the types of occupations held by Spanish-surnamed individuals during the first three decades of the twentieth century, which reflected a shrinking of the white collar and growth of low blue-collar sectors. In the interwar years, the occupational patterns of Puerto Ricans had much in common with that of other foreign-born whites, such as the Italians, one of the new immigrant groups that arrived in Philadelphia in this time period. During the Great Depression, however, a dramatic and destructive shift began to take place in the occupational patterns of Puerto Ricans in Philadelphia.

By 1930, Puerto Ricans' labor participation began to look more similar to that of African Americans than any other group in the city. During the 1930s, Spanish-speakers' level of unemployment was only surpassed by that of blacks. As people of color, Puerto Ricans and other racially mixed Latinos also proved difficult to incorporate into all sectors of the economy. In the case of blacks, whose relative numbers continued to increase due to migration from the South, their skin color

Table 2: Occupation Structure for Spanish-surnamed individuals in Philadelphia, Selective years from 1910–1936

	1910	%	1920	%	1930	%	1936	%
High White Collar								
Professionals	14	8	27	14	35	11	33	10
Proprietorial	22	12	16	8	18	6	12	4
Low-White Collar	16	9	10	5	32	10	33	10
High Blue-Collar								
(Skilled)	43	24	42	22	62	20	58	18
Low Blue-Collar								
(Semi-skilled)	27	15	21	11	28	9	22	7
(Unskilled)	24	13	30	15	53	17	35	11
Domestic & Personal								
Service	3	1	2	1	8	3	8	3
Unspecified	32	18	46	24	73	24	124	37
Total	181	100	194	100	309	100	325	100

* Source: *Boyd's Philadelphia City Directories*, 1910, 1919–1920, 1930; *Polk's Philadelphia City Directory*, 1935–1936, Temple University Urban Archives.

and their poor and working-class backgrounds prevented them from this incorporation. Increasingly, blacks became more entrenched in the unskilled sector of the Philadelphia economy. Puerto Ricans, in addition to their mixed racial background, also spoke a different language and exhibited a foreign culture, which they continued to sustain in their new environment. Yet, despite some differences between blacks and Puerto Ricans in the 1930s, the similarities were stronger. Both African Americans and Puerto Ricans were U.S. citizens, although this fact did not seem to increase the chances of improving their lot.

Spanish Surname Occupational Structure in Philadelphia, 1910–1940

During the interwar period, Puerto Ricans initially gained a foothold in some professional sectors and skilled labor jobs, particularly in the 1920s. Progressively, as the Great Depression wreaked its havoc and World War II pushed full employment and expanded, once again the need for unskilled labor, Puerto Ricans along with blacks filled the lower rungs of employment. In addition, during the first half of the twentieth century, the overall labor participation rate of Puerto Ricans in Philadelphia declined in a substantial manner.

The initial labor participation data for those with Spanish surnames was gleaned from selective dates. The information came from city directories. This data does not list individuals by nationalities only surname. The next set of data presents a sample of Spanish speaking workers in Philadelphia. During the first four decades of the twentieth century, the occupational structure of Spanish surnamed workers in Philadelphia reflected a continuous appearance within working-class, blue-collar categories (see Table 2). Labor participation for Hispanics in this time period decreased from 82.3 percent in 1910 to 62.1 percent by 1936. The number of blue-collar, Puerto Rican and other Latino workers, in this period, decreased from 52 percent in 1910 to 35.5 percent in 1936. In the white-collar sectors, their overall percentage declined substantially from 23.8 percent in 1910 to 17.9 percent in 1936. The most dramatic changes in the overall occupational picture of these workers throughout this time period, however, was the steady increase in the number of people listed in Philadelphia City Directories without an occupation. The occupation of these individuals was unspecified and was, in all probability, unskilled laborers.[1]

Samples gleaned from the Philadelphia City Directories for selective years between 1910 and 1936, note how Hispanics fared in white and blue collar employment. Between 1910 and 1920, for instance, the two occupational sectors for this group most impacted were: 1- professionals who experienced a modest increase and 2- Semi-skilled blue-collar workers who experienced a slight decrease in this period. Of the fourteen professionals listed in the city directory in 1910, none appeared among the twenty-seven listed in 1920. What happened to those professionals listed in 1910 is unclear? One possible explanation is that some of those professionals listed in 1910 died during the course of the next decade. Some of those professionals may have also moved out of the city or migrated elsewhere, possibly to New York where there existed greater employment possibilities during the decade. However, despite the fact that the professionals listed in the 1910 City Directory did not reappear in 1920, the increase in total numbers of this category (from 14 in 1910 to 27 in 1920) points to the possibility that, as the general Spanish-speaking population increased during the decade, so did the need for professional services. Included in the professional group in 1920 were six dentists and four physicians. In addition, the increase of professionals that appear listed in the Philadelphia City Directory in 1920 suggests an increase in migration in this period. At least two professionals listed in 1920 had migrated to the United States during the decade between 1910 and 1920. One of those migrants was Dr. José DeCelis, the Puerto Rican dentist mentioned in prior chapters and the other was Dr. Pedro Carreras, another Puerto Rican, a physician and close friend of Tomas Rodriguez. Together, DeCelis and Carreras are representative of a small but growing professional class among Puerto Ricans in the city in this period.[2]

The biggest decline occurred in the semi-skilled ranks as reflected in the sample of Spanish-surname cigar makers in the city. In 1910 there were 19 Spanish-surname cigar makers listed in the City Directory, in 1920 there were only 6. This decrease can be explained by an overall shrinkage in the hand-rolled manufacturing of cigars in the industry. The increasing use of factory-style cigar production beginning in the early twentieth century and wide use of a cigar making machine after 1910 drove many male cigar makers from the industry. Some of those cigar makers, like Saturnino Dones after almost 25years of living in Philadelphia moved to New York City's bourgeoning Puerto Rican community in East Harlem and became a *bodeguero* but the majority did not. Many displaced cigar makers may have wound up as unskilled laborers. This last category did show a moderate increase from 12 in 1910 to 19 in 1920.[3]

During the pre-and post-Great Depression period, the vast majority of Hispanic workers in this sample remained predominantly in blue-collar jobs. Qualitative changes in the occupational structures of Puerto Ricans changed little in the first three decades of the twentieth century. Quantitatively, there was a change due to the influx of workers during the World War I years (1914–1918), especially during 1917 and 1918. One area in which this is evident is in the high blue-collar (skilled) category. In this category, although the percentages decreased (23.8 to 21.7 percent) between 1910 and 1920, the overall numbers remained fairly even (43 to 42). This was probably a reflection of World War I employment patterns, for example during the war there were Puerto Ricans and other Latinos living in Spring Garden who worked as machinists (skilled, blue-collar) for the Baldwin Locomotive Works Company, and in the ship yards, among other war related industries. For example, by 1917, as the U.S. entered the World War, Saturnino Dones found himself working as a "filer" for the Eddystone Rifle Works, a defense industry.[46] In 1917, Antonio Malpica registered for the draft. Unlike Dones, he was still employed as a cigar maker and working at a cigar factory located at 23 Market Street on June 5, 1917 the day he signed up. Malpica was listed as "negro" medium height, medium built, brown eyes and black hair. But, by October 1918, while the country was still at war, Malpica joined the U.S. Navy. The patriotic fever also was caught by professionals as well. Jose DeCelis, newly graduating from Temple University also enlisted in the U.S. Navy on July 24, 1918 was well as Pedro Carreras, a student of medicine.[5]

Despite the fact that the percentages in this category continued to decrease (18.5 percent in 1930 to 17.9 percent in 1936) the overall numbers were higher in those years than in 1920. Overall, however, variations did occur in the distribution of Spanish-surname workers in the high white-collar sectors between 1910 and 1920. In particular, two categories experienced change over the decade: 1-the percentage of Latino professionals increased from 13.9 percent in 1920, up from 7.7 percent in 1910, and 2-the percentage of proprietors decreased from 12.2 to 8.3 percent (U.S. Department of Commerce 1920; *Philadelphia City Directory* 1910, 1919–1920, 1930, 1935–1936).[6]

This data indicates the constriction or expansion of particular industries in the city and its impact on employment options for Hispanics in this time period. In 1910, the most prevalent occupations of this group are listed in Table 3. The seventy individuals listed in the table represent almost half (49 percent) of the sample of working Hispanics in 1910 utilized to construct this table. The largest number in the group, cigar makers (19) indicates that this was still an important trade for this group in Philadelphia. It is interesting to note that all nineteen-cigar makers in this group were men. In 1910, cigar making was still an important trade in Philadelphia. In addition, by 1910, the process of feminization of cigar making in Puerto Rico was in full swing, thereby, prompting displaced male cigar makers to migrate to the United States. This was the case of Antonio Malpica. In 1910, he was a cigar maker residing in Old San Juan, the co-

Table 3: Selected Occupations and Highest Frequencies for Spanish-surname, Philadelphia, 1910 and 1920

Occupation	1910	1920
Cigar Maker	19	6
Laborer	12	19
Cigars (Proprietor)	9	9
Clerk	10	6
Barber	6	
Manager	6	
Grocer	5	4
Machinist	4	12
Dentist		6
Formen		6
US Navy		5
Physician		4
Salesman		4
Total	71	81

Total sample for 1910, 187 Spanish-surname (150 men and 30 women); Total Sample for 1920, 204 Spanish-surname (162 men and 42 women)

* Source: *Boyd's Philadelphia City Directories*, 1910, 1919–1920

lonial sector of the capital of Puerto Rico. But, by 1913, he was in Philadelphia working in a cigar factory. Together with Spanish-speaking owners of cigar making operations in Philadelphia (9), the two groups made up about one-fifth (18.8 percent), of all occupations held by Hispanics in this period. Of the nine owners of cigar making shops, Latinas owned two of them (*Boyd's Philadelphia City Directory* 1910).[7]

Other prominent occupations of Latino residents of Philadelphia in 1910 included laborers (12); clerks (9); barbers and managers (6); grocers (5) and machinists (4). Unfortunately, the City Directory very often did not list the place of occupation, so that it is difficult to analyze, for instance, where clerks and managers were employed. Thus, the data does not permit a more complete picture with respect to place of employment of white and blue-collar workers. For barbers and grocers, however, two important endeavors in ethnic communities, most of their business addresses are listed. Almost all barbers and grocers had their place of business located within the Spanish-speaking enclaves. This fact is significant in that, traditionally, grocery stores in particular, played an important social role in the Puerto Rican community. Aside from providing special products particular to the community, the grocery store or "bodega" was a place of interaction—sharing of information such as job opportunities as well as a place to speak Spanish.

By 1920, Hispanics had expanded their job categories in Philadelphia as denoted by their respective frequencies. The biggest increase in jobs between 1910 and 1920, occurred in two categories: laborers and machinists. During the war, machinists made up an important labor category especially in armament manufacturing. Also, during war periods, jobs for unskilled laborers were generally in great demand. Progressively, however, the laborer category became more representative of Puerto Rican job categories beyond the war years. Also reflective of wartime employment were the five Spanish-speakers listed as members of the U.S. Navy in addition to two more Latinos listed as members of the U.S. Army, all residents of the Pan-Hispanic enclaves in the city (*Boyd's Philadelphia City Directory* 1910).

Another notable change in the occupational categories in 1920, was in the white-collar sector, especially professionals. Job listings of Spanish-surname in the 1920 City Directory included the names of four Latino physicians and six dentists. Although the number of clerks decreased from 1910 and 1920, from nine to six, there were, in addition four salesmen, increasing this low white-collar category among this group, in the city at the time. The most significant drop in job categories 1910 and 1920 was among cigar makers. This group shrunk from nineteen to six during the decade. More importantly, cigar making would never recover its prominence as an area of employment for Spanish-speakers. Part of the reason for the decline in cigar makers was that in 1919 the tobacco manufacturing industry nationwide introduced the cigar making machine. The implementation of the machine spelled, almost instantly, the end of the hand-rolled cigar as a commodity, and began the steady decline of this once, male-dominated craft. After 1920, greater numbers of cigars were produced by machines operated by women. Correspondingly, all six Spanish-speaking cigar makers listed in the Philadelphia City Directory in 1920 were women. As we will see, although cigar making decreased significantly, it did not totally disappear as an occupation among Spanish-speaking men. One reason why male cigar making continued to exist, especially in small, community-based operations was due to incessant migration among this group (*Boyd's Philadelphia City Directory* 1930).

By 1930, blue-collar Spanish-speakers made up 37 percent of the group. The numbers for Spanish-surname workers in Philadelphia began to decrease once the

Table 4: Selected Occupations and Highest Frequencies for Spanish-surname, Philadelphia, 1930 and 1936

Occupation	1930	1936
Laborer	42	10
Clerk	17	12
Salesman	11	10
Tailor	9	6
Barber	9	
Machinist	7	8
Cigar Maker	6	6
Cigars (Proprietor)	6	4
Waiter	5	4
Engineer	4	6
Grocer	4	4
Teacher	3	6
Helper	3	6
Baker		7
Painter		5
Fireman		4
Chef		4
Total	123	108

* Source: *Boyd's Philadelphia City Directory*, 1930; *Polk's City Directory*, 1935-36

Great Depression hit. This loss was consistent throughout the 1930s. The only sector to recuperate significant numbers of workers in the post-Depression era was the low blue-collar sector. This sector began to pick up ground during the labor shortage period of the Second World War. Once the war ended, Puerto Ricans began to occupy low blue-collar employment in higher percentages than before the war (*Boyd's Philadelphia City Directory* 1930).

The twelve categories listed comprised 46.9 percent of all jobs held by this group in 1930. The most dramatic change occurred in the occupation of laborers. The total number of laborers jumped from 19 in 1920 to 42 in 1930. This was a reflection of increased labor segmentation, meaning more openings for unskilled labor in this period. As native-born white, and increasingly, foreign-born white workers moved up from unskilled to semi-skilled jobs and from these to blue-collar skilled ranks, more jobs became available in the lowest rungs of the unskilled category. Many of these unskilled jobs were filled by the Puerto Rican newcomers. Among the semi-skilled, although cigar making continued to expand into large factories, the hand-rolled craft continued to exist among a small group of Latinos. Of the six cigar makers listed in the Philadelphia City Directory in 1930, five of them are men. In 1930, approximately 20 percent of men who were employed were laborers or worked in factories; another five percent were cigar makers or machinists. Of the 50 women Spanish-surname women that appeared about half of them had an occupation listed. These women can be divided up, mostly into two groups: 1-low white-collar (12) and 2-low blue-collar (9), including two cigar makers. There was also one physician listed among the group of women (Chenault 1938: 70–1; *Boyd's Philadelphia City Directory* 1930).

By 1930, there was also a significant increase in low white-collar participation rates of Spanish-surname workers. Between 1920 and 1930, the percentage of white-collar workers among this group increased from 5.5 percent to 9.6 percent, almost double. Most of these employees were clerks or in sales. Latino men outnumbered Latina women in these ranks, twenty-four to four. On the other hand, the 1930 numbers reflect a decrease in high white-collar occupations. The proprietorial sector decreased in percentages from a high 8.3 percent in 1920 to 5.4 percent in 1930, although the relative numbers did not change that much. The professional sector also experienced a dramatic downturn in this period. Professional Spanish-surname numbers decreased from 12.2 percent in 1910 to 10.6 percent in 1920, to only 5.1 percent in 1930. It is not clear what happened to the professional ranks.

Although, they tended to reside in many parts of the city, Latino workers were still concentrated in a few specific areas of Philadelphia. For instance, the largest portion, 58 percent, lived in Southwark in South Philadelphia, a traditional ethnic neighborhood. Forty-five percent of the blue-collar workers were concentrated in Southwark, with thirty-one percent of the white-collar workers residing in West Philadelphia. In the West Philadelphia section of the city is where many low white-collar and professionals in the city were moving to in this period (Miller et al. 1983: 433–4).

Despite limited success in employment and economic security in Philadelphia, Puerto Ricans continued to migrate to the city in the 1930s and 1940s. Despite limited skills or industrial training, limited or little dominance of the English language and, in some instances, poor health they continued to migrate. Not even the prejudice and discrimination they faced deterred them, in any significant way, from migrating from the island to Philadelphia. Two stories illustrate the climate Puerto Ricans found in Philadelphia: that of Tomasita Romero and Carmen Aponte. In interviews conducted in the 1990s both women shared their respective experiences looking for housing and work in the city. On more than one occasion, Tomasita and Carmen were turned away from rental opportunities because of their "color" because they were darker skinned Puerto Ricans. Yet, when their respective husbands, who looked "white" but had heavy accents, were the ones who went looking for the same housing both were offered the same apartments their wives had been denied. Mr. Romero and Mr. Aponte were probably perceived to be foreign-born white men.[8] All of these limitations appear to have been overlooked and overcome, in part, because economic conditions on the island were worse at the time. On the whole, however, Philadelphia Spanish-speakers, especially those who migrated during the 1920–1930 period seemed to have improved their lot, somewhat. This was especially true for some of the second generation who spoke English. But, most Puerto Ricans and other Spanish-speakers, in general continued to labor, when at all, in blue-collar jobs.[9]

During the Depression years, employment opportunities for Puerto Ricans were drastically reduced. Few newcomers made Philadelphia their home in the early part of this period. Between the years 1931 and 1934, almost 9,000 Puerto Ricans left the United States and returned to Puerto Rico. This number represented 20 percent of Puerto Ricans living in the United States at the time. Though many left, argues U.S.-born, Puerto Rican historian Virginia Sanchez-Korrol, the avenues of formal and informal communications between Puerto Ricans in the United States and those on the island, what she calls the "family intelligence network", kept potential migrants abreast of the varying employment situation in the north. By mid decade, Puerto Rican migration picked up again. Between 1934 and 1940, more than 17,000 Puerto Ricans moved to the United States. For Philadelphia, this meant that the enclaves continued to grow despite economic adversity. One explanation for this apparent contradiction is that during the Depression, unemployment in Puerto Rico rose to

37 percent. This factor combined with an increase in employment in the agricultural phase of sugar production, the largest employer on the island, coupled with a reduction in the length of the workday resulted in the effective reduction of real wages. Also, the increase in federal programs in the United States by the mid-1930s offered a more positive option for Puerto Ricans to leave rather than remain on the island, hence an increase in migration (Miller et al. 1983: 6; Sánchez-Korrol 1994: 31; Centro de Estudios Puertorriqueños 1979: 112; Chenault 1938: 7).

In the years between 1930 and 1936, the Spanish-speaking population of the city was highly mobile. Many left the city after 1930. Of more than 330 Spanish-speakers listed as residents in the Philadelphia City Directory in 1930, only one quarter of them were still residing in Philadelphia six years later. According to the city directory for 1936, 37 percent of Spanish-speakers appeared to have no employment. The figures provided by the directories indicate that the unemployment rate among Spanish-speakers during the Depression was somewhat higher than the rest of the city. Unemployment rates in Philadelphia in 1936 stood at 30.1 percent city-wide (*Boyd's Philadelphia City Directory* 1930; *Polk's City Directory*). For Mary Rodriguez there was a moment in the late 1930s when her husband Tomas almost lost his job as a drug tester when his company began to lay-off employees. What saved Tomas' job was another Puerto Rican, Armando Maldonado who convinced the company to lay him off instead arguing that Tomas was married with three children and he (Maldonado) was single and had no children! Sixty plus years later, Mary and her daughter Emma were extremely grateful and remembered this friend's sacrifice (Rodriguez 1999; Pajil 1999).

Those Puerto Ricans that remained in Philadelphia during the Depression, and were fortunate enough to be employed were concentrated in blue-collar jobs. Many foreign-born whites, or their children who were more experienced with the English language and American customs, had also progressed to blue-collar skilled positions during the 1920s and found themselves unemployed in the 1930s and competing for menial jobs as well (Sánchez-Korrol 1994: 32).

By 1936, the last year for which the Philadelphia City Directory data is available, the overall job opportunities of Hispanics had decreased from a high of 82.3 percent (all categories included) in 1910, to 63 percent. Citywide, that year, 69.1 percent of employable persons in Philadelphia were working. Puerto Ricans and other Spanish-speakers had a higher unemployment rate during the Depression than that of native-born and foreign-born whites respectively, but not as low as that of blacks. Unemployment figures for blacks in this time period reflect that 52.1 percent were employed while 47.9 percent were unemployed. Workers in the fifteen categories listed accounted for 45.8 percent of all employed Hispanics in Philadelphia in 1936 (Franklin 1979: 106–7).

The biggest drop from 1930 occurred among the laborer occupational cluster. This unskilled group was significantly affected, in part because there was enormous competition across the city for jobs in this category. Increased migration from Puerto Rico after 1934 also contributed to swelling the ranks of potential workers who competed for the few available jobs. In addition, there was an increase in the number of women in the labor force, especially in the unskilled ranks. For instance, eight out the ten individuals listed in the 1936 City Directory as helpers were women (*Polk's Philadelphia City Directory* 1935–1936).

During the first three decades of the twentieth century, Puerto Rican migrants expanded the types of occupations that were available to them. However, more and more, those opportunities arose within the low blue-collar ranks. By the middle of the Depression, many Puerto Rican workers were unskilled laborers. In addition, more women joined the employment ranks, some in low white-collar work. But, for the most part, Puerto Rican migrants in this time period held the most menial and difficult jobs and were relegated to the lower rungs of employment in the city.

Comparative Occupational Structure for Native-born Whites, Foreign-born, Italians and blacks and Hispanics in Philadelphia, 1930

For Puerto Ricans and other Latinos and African Americans, the labor segmentation that would be a key feature of their respective employment options in the Post-WW II era actually began to take shape in the early decades of the twentieth century. Industrial and labor needs of Philadelphia attracted many different types of workers. As industrialization expanded at the end of the nineteenth century, more and more workers from Europe, Asia and Latin America were attracted. Invariably, labor-intensive industries like the railroads, in constant need of unskilled laborers, especially took it upon themselves to recruit workers outside of the city. This was the case for Italians, blacks, as well as Puerto Ricans.

Foreign-born immigrants and black migrants also found their occupational opportunities limited in this time period. More and more job opportunities that opened up were located in the local economy's white-collar sector. The largest expansion occurred in the professional ranks or in service categories. Faced with discrimination, language difficulties and limited educational backgrounds, few of these groups worked in these jobs (Hershberg et al. 1981: 474). Puerto Ricans in 1930 reflected more similarities with foreign-born whites than with any other group. In terms of low white-collar and high blue-collar percentages, Puerto Ricans and other Latinos were more similar to foreign-born whites in Philadelphia, 9.6 to 10.9 and 18.5 to 23.2 percent respectively. Also, the percentage of unskilled laborers among Hispanics (15.8 in 1930), was closest by comparison to the general percentage of foreign-born white laborers (20.6 percent) at the time. In terms of blacks and Hispanics, the only category in which there seemed to be some similarity, albeit slightly different, was in the percentages in the unskilled ranks. Black unskilled workers in 1930 made up 68.9 percent of the group. Although Puerto Rican unskilled workers were only 15.8 percent of their respective group, this figure represented the second largest among Latinos. The percentage of Italians workers who were clerks in sales and other jobs in this category in 1930 was only 4.5 percent, blacks were 3.3 percent. Similarly, Italian skilled workers were only 7 percent and blacks, 5.8 percent of this occupational group.

None of Philadelphia's major industries employed large numbers of unskilled laborers. That was the case of employers such as textiles and garment manufacturers, printing and publishing, and metal manufacturing of hardware and machine shops. Few industries of this sort moved into the city. Tens of thousands of Jews and Italians made a living in the needle trades (garment industry), the Poles did not. Perhaps, as Golab argues, this was because Poles perceived needlework as women's work. Male Poles preferred physical work and this kept them out of the industry.[4] Since Poles were excluded from skilled and female labor markets, they were concentrated in unskilled labor. Here, they competed with blacks, Irish-Americans and Italians. Polish workers in Philadelphia were normally confined to the secondary labor market where blacks predominated. Like blacks, Poles were the last hired and first fired. Though outnumbered 8–1 in this labor sector, Poles made gains in the period, and in fact, shared similar occupational patterns with blacks, such as domestic service, a mainstay of both black and Polish women in this time period (Golab 1977: 108).

Poles did not compete with Italians or Jews in the artisan or merchant sectors. Italians and Jews had been doing this type of work for centuries before immigration, the Poles had not. In the heavier manual and unskilled occupations, Jews and Poles were never competitors. For the most part, Polish, Jewish and Italians operated in different sectors of occupations (Golab 1977: 109).

Italians secured dominance in some of the unskilled labor categories. Due to their *padrone* system, a built-in brokerage network, Italians were able to monopolize sectors such as railroad and public works. Between 1900 and 1930, Italians in Philadelphia worked in substantial numbers as seasonal farm laborers in New Jersey. In addition, although not in large numbers, Italian women also worked in the city's garment district, though Jewish women predominated in this industry. At the end of the farming season, Italians were then employed to work in construction gangs throughout the city (Varbero 1974: 122–3).

Italian-American historian Richard A. Varbero indicates that Italian immigrants did not work in very many industrial factories in the city. The exception to Italian

Table 5: Comparative Occupational Structure, Philadelphia, Native-born White, Foreign-born White, Italians, Blacks and Latinos, 1930

OCCUPATION	NATIVE-BORN WHITE	%	FOREIGN-BORN WHITE	%
High White Collar	44,399	8	7,243	4
Professionals	43,827	8	28,122	14
Low-White Collar	174,389	32	22,084	11
High Blue-Collar				
(Skilled)	78,039	14	47,259	23
Low Blue-Collar				
(Semi-skilled)	158,450	30	56,672	28
(Unskilled)	46,357	8	41,912	21
Unspecified				
Total	545,481	100	203,292	100

OCCUPATION	ITALIANS	%	BLACKS	%	LATINOS	%
High White Collar	1,125	4	2,347	2	35	11
Professionals	8,651	32	2,304	2	18	5
Low-White Collar	1,568	6	3,978	3	33	10
High Blue-Collar						
(Skilled)	2,427	9	6,937	6	58	18
Low Blue-Collar						
(Semi-skilled)	34	21,559	18	22	7	28
(Unskilled)	7	81,565	69	35	11	21
Unspecified	2,123	8			124	38
Total	27,103	100	118,690	100	325*	100

Sources: *Fifteenth United States Census Schedule*, 1930, Social Economic Grouping of Gainful Workers, Philadelphia, p. 276; Richard A. Varbero, "Urbanization and Acculturation: Philadelphia's Southern Italians, 1918-1932," p. 136; Boyd's *Philadelphia City Directory*, 1930

* This number represents one hundred percent of the sample; it does not reflect the total number of Spanish-speakers in the city at the time.

labor participation in industry was in the garment district. There was a significant presence of Italians, men and women, especially those that had skills in tailoring and as seamstresses. Most of the jobs held by Italians in this time period were semi-skilled in a variety of operative positions. In 1930, the semi-skilled category accounted for one quarter of all jobs held by Italians in Philadelphia (see Table 5). The other large occupational category of Italian employment in the city in 1930 was in "proprietorial." However, as Varbero points out, many Italians in this category were small-time peddlers, merchants, and retailers. (Varbero 1974: 128).

Prior to World War I, Philadelphia contained the second largest African American population in the North. Pennsylvania was the first state in the North to import southern black labor migrants, in large numbers, during the First World War. The Pennsylvania Railroad Company claimed credit for initiating this importation through its project of free transportation. Between May 1916 and July 1917, the Pennsylvania Railroad carried more than 13,000 African Americans North. In the same period, the Erie Railroad Company also transported an additional 9,000 black laborers to the North. These labor migrants, along with countless other volunteer migrants, upon learning about job opportunities from friends and family, also headed north. This contributed to the growth of the black population in Philadelphia during this period (Hardy 1989: 1, 75–6).

Blacks were excluded from the textile and garment industries, two of the city's largest employers at that time. For instance, in 1915, blacks made up 6 percent of Philadelphia's population, yet they only accounted for 339 out of 65,517 manufacturing jobs, and only 154 out of 38,458 textile jobs. Notwithstanding these exclusionary practices, blacks made inroads in several wartime industries like Midvale Steel. Increased labor shortages during World War I contributed to a partial opening of industrial jobs for blacks in Philadelphia (Hardy 1989: 6–7; Banner-Haley 1992: 180).

The end of World War I, however, had a negative impact on the Philadelphia war industries. Cutbacks in government contracts meant cutbacks in the workforce. The negative effects were also felt in the local black labor force. The Disston Saws Works, a premier war industry, had expanded its workforce by 1,000 between 1916 and 1918. Due to losses of war contracts, Disston laid-off 700 workers within the first year after the end of the war. The cutbacks in the labor force were accompanied by a re-imposition of racial presumptions in the city. Exclusionary labor practices against blacks in Philadelphia lasted well into World War II when the federal government forced the inclusion of blacks into industries that received federal contracts (Hardy 1992: 94, 115).

The period after World War I and right on into the Great Depression impacted negatively the small, but significant, black middle class as well as the many unskilled black

Table 6: Comparative Occupation Structure for Puerto Ricans and other Latinos, Philadelphia, 1910–1940

OCCUPATION	1910				1920			
	LATINOS	%	PUERTO RICANS	%	LATINOS	%	PUERTO RICANS	%
High White Collar								
Professionals	14	7.7	1	1.2	27	13.8	20	6.8
Proprietorial	22	12.2	2	2.4	16	8.2	8	2.7
Low-White Collar	16	8.7	2	2.4	10	5.1	12	4
High Blue-Collar								
(Skilled)	43	23.8	1	1.3	42	21.7	10	3.4
Low Blue-Collar								
(Semi-skilled)	27	15	11	13.4	21	11	56	19.2
(Unskilled)	24	13.3	7	9	30	15.5	51	17.5
Domestic/Personal								
Service	3	1.7	2	2.4	2	1	4	1.4
Unspecified	32	17.6	56	68	46	23.7	131	4.5
Total	181	100	82	100	194	100	292	100

OCCUPATION	1930				1940	
	LATINOS	%	PUERTO RICANS	%	PUERTO RICANS	%
High White Collar						
Professionals	35	11.2	30	11.2	13	4.3
Proprietorial	18	5.8	2	1	9	3
Low-White Collar	32	10.4	20	7.5	36	12
High Blue-Collar						
(Skilled)	62	20	17	6.4	20	6.7
Low Blue-Collar						
(Semi-skilled)	28	9	61	22.8	58	19.2
(Unskilled)	53	17	62	23.3	59	19.5
Domestic/Personal						
Service	8	2.5	1	0		
Unspecified	73	24	74	28	107	35.4
Total	309	100	267	100	302	100

Source: For Latinos, the sample numbers came from the *Boyd's Philadelphia City Directories for 1910, 1919–20 and 1930*, Temple University Urban Archives. The sample numbers for Puerto Ricans were drawn from the Manuscript Census for 1910, 1920, 1930 and 1940

laborers. In the latter part of the 1920s and throughout the 1930s, employment opportunities for blacks were drastically reduced. Those blacks that were employed during the Depression were overwhelmingly unskilled labors—see Table 5. In 1930, low blue-collar jobs accounted for 87 percent of blacks that were employed in Philadelphia. By 1933, almost 52 percent of employable persons in black Philadelphia were unemployed. For the same period, the foreign-born white population had an unemployment rate of 28.4 percent, while the native-born white population's unemployment rate was 30.6 percent. That year, the citywide unemployment rate was 46 percent, the highest during all the years of the Great Depression (Gregg 1993: 3; Banner-Haley 1992: 184).

Cigar making was one of the few industries in Philadelphia's manufacturing economy in which black women, in particular, found employment other than domestic service. This was, however, unhealthy work. It was also amongst the poorest paying, most racist and most unpleasant occupations in the city. The city was cited in 1907 for having the most decrepit and unsanitary tobacco factories in the country. Black women, who still made up 20 percent of workers in cigar making in 1940, were relegated to the worst type of labor conditions in the industry: stripping. Stripping was the lowest paying work in the industry. It was monotonous, unhealthy and a soggy process often performed in wet, dark basements. Almost 400 out of 443 black women at the Bayuk were employed as strippers (those who stripped the main stem from the tobacco leaf). In 1927, of the 2,500 black women employed in the cigar industry were almost all strippers (Hardy 1989: 107; Paul 1940: 43, 51–3).

Occupational Patterns for Puerto Ricans during World War II and Beyond
By the early 1940s, employment opportunities for Puerto Ricans and other Spanish-speakers began to change again in Philadelphia and vicinity. In the early months of 1940, unemployment in U.S. cities exceeded official rates in Puerto Rico, but by 1943, with the country fully engaged in World War II, full employment had been reached in the United States. Puerto Rican labor migration to Philadelphia contributed to, and increased its numbers in this period. Large-scale labor recruitment became a significant part of employment opportunities in the United States for women, blacks and Puerto Ricans as they were all actively recruited during the war. U.S.-born Puerto Rican historian Carmen T. Whalen has documented the recruitment of Puerto Rican contract laborers to the Philadelphia region in this time period. Labor shortages in key war industries in the Philadelphia-Camden area prompted recruitment efforts that brought several thousand more Puerto Rican workers to the city and the region to work in food production and railroads. For the most part, work in the food plants, for which Puerto Ricans and blacks were recruited, were among to lowest paid unskilled labor. In addition, this recruitment

effort indirectly prompted several thousands more Puerto Rican workers to migrate on their own to Philadelphia and vicinity to work in agricultural and industrial jobs. Many like Marcelo Benitez, Juan Canales and others moved to Philadelphia (Sánchez-Korrol 1994: 3; Whalen 1994: chapter 4; *Business Week* 1944a, 1944b).[10]

The period between 1920 and 1945 represents a major transition in the occupational patterns of Puerto Ricans and other Spanish-speakers in Philadelphia compared to other groups. In that twenty-five year period, the Latino population went from being significantly to overwhelmingly blue-collar. In 1930, 42.7 percent of Latinos were blue-collar workers; by 1950, it was 80 percent. In addition, there was a dramatic shift within the blue-collar ranks. In 1930, 18.5 percent of Puerto Ricans were skilled, blue-collar workers. By 1950, male Puerto Rican skilled workers made up only 7.8 percent and women a mere 2.9 percent of the group. Meanwhile, the number of Puerto Rican men in service and operator/laborer positions made up 72.2 percent of the group (*Boyd's Philadelphia City Directory* 1930; Whalen 2000: 126).

Some economists argue that the Great Depression startled, temporarily the nation's economy, in Philadelphia it proved to be a watershed. The city's industrial base began to decline during this period and manufacturing was its biggest victim. This economic shift impacted significantly upon the city's black and Puerto Rican population. Although blacks were initially excluded from many manufacturing jobs, by 1950, 28.2 percent of black males and 21.9 percent of black females, respectively, were engaged in manufacturing jobs. In the same year, 26.6 percent of Puerto Rican males and 53.0 percent of Puerto Rican females also worked in manufacturing (Adams et al. 1991: 14; Whalen 2000: 126).

Between 1930 and 1945, occupational patterns for Puerto Ricans and blacks reflected a process of concentration in sectors of the economy that were doomed by deinvestment patterns of the business class. Automation increased volumes of production, and manufacturer's greater efforts to market their products stimulated service employment in which few Puerto Ricans and blacks labored. The growth of industrialization in other countries after World War II also undercut U.S. manufacturing. In addition to the national and local economic shifts, an increase in housing segregation in Philadelphia combined with the aforementioned economic dislocation of blacks and Puerto Ricans helped consolidate each group's ghettos. These patterns locked Puerto Ricans into occupations which had very little future in the post-industrial economy.

Conclusion

During these early decades, many Puerto Ricans landed jobs in industries that produced non-durable goods. These were some of the industries that were eventually the most affected by the economic shift from an industrial to a post-industrial economy in Philadelphia. The smaller industries required lower capital investments and generally paid lower wages. Those characteristics allowed these firms to relocate more easily—something they eventually did when they abandoned the city for friendlier and cheaper labor. By comparison, durable goods such as machinery, automobiles, washers and construction required more investments and consequently were harder to relocate, thus many remained in the city for a longer period of time. Philadelphia's greater dependency on a non-durable manufacturing economy, up to 30 percent of its economy by the 1940s, spelled disaster in the post-World War II period. Philadelphia's dependence on an infrastructure that relied heavily on non-durable goods negatively impacted Puerto Ricans and other Spanish-speakers who labored in these industries, especially in cigar making. Their occupational choices also shifted, and as the economy changed, so did their options (Adams 1991: 39, chapter 5).

Puerto Rican migrants in Philadelphia experienced a segmented labor market in the inter-war period. The occupational patterns of Puerto Ricans, in this time period, are also an indicator of their plight in post-industrial Philadelphia. They caught the initial wave of de-industrialization that solidified following World War I. Their labor participation in the city also reveals their proletarianization; a process begun in Puerto Rico that continued in Philadelphia. For the most part, Puerto Ricans and other Spanish-speakers' occupational patterns before 1945 reveal that they labored largely in the blue-collar sectors of the city's economy. The post-industrial poverty and economic dislocation of Puerto Ricans and blacks in Philadelphia, after 1945, has its roots in the economic transformation of the city during the previous decades.

As some of these groups progressed, the working-class enclaves established by Puerto Ricans and other Spanish-speakers were oftentimes-shared spaces with other ethnic and racial groups, particularly those considered "white", like the Poles and the Italians, they moved to other parts of the city and surrounding suburbs, uninhibited by discriminatory housing and occupational policies of the times. Puerto Ricans who stayed behind, and those who continued the migratory process from the island to Philadelphia, built their enclaves into a community. The implications for the labor market were one of increased secondary and tertiary sectors, in which many of the workers increasingly were black and Puerto Rican.

The types of jobs that Puerto Ricans held during the first half of the twentieth century helps to paint a picture of how this labor migrant group opened up occupational and residential space in an industrial city, like Philadelphia, that was undergoing the earliest stages of industrial decline and economic transformation to a post-industrial base. This economic conversion presents a framework for comprehending what jobs

Spanish-speakers held in this period as well as their labor segmentation from certain types of employment. This is an important backdrop for placing the Puerto Rican community development process within the broader confines of a racially divided city.

It is within the population shift and economic restructuring in Philadelphia in the early twentieth century that Puerto Ricans organized and built the community institutions to sustain them as they incorporated into the city. The next chapter explores the pre-war residents and how they built upon the institutional support organizations. A process the Pan-Hispanic enclaves reached to support each other and consolidated the settlements of Spring Garden, Northern Liberties and Southwark into a vibrant Puerto Rican community in Philadelphia.

Image 14. International Workers Order, Spanish Lodge, Philadelphia Chapter dance 1940, provides a glimpse into the diversity of the community. IWO Spanish Lodge nationally was led by Puerto Rican Jesus Colon out of New York.

Image 15. Mexican Independence Day Celebration, 1940. The Mexican Consulate Office was very active among the Spanish-speaking enclaves throughout t the Interwar years. The Anahuac Association was sponsored by the International Institute, a group supportive of all immigrant communities in Philadelphia since the 1920s.

La Fraternal Dance Flyer, Philadelphia, 1945

265-

Sociedad Fraternal

Hispano-Americana de Filadelfia

++

GRAND SHOW and DAN

Saturday, March 17, 1945

at BOSLOVER HALL

701 Pine Street

By popular demand, the One - Act Comedy
"LA BARBERIA DE TRIANA",
written by A. Fernandez and E. Castro, will be shown
by the Artistic Group of this Society.

-CAST

Don Cristobal	Antonio Fernandez
Parrita	Enrique Castro
Posturitas	Abran Benhayon
Rosita	Inez Larrea
Leganitas	Jose Echevarria
Currito	Pablo Larrea
Caracol	Hilario Ramos

MUSIC BY A LATIN-AMERICAN ORCHESTRA FROM NEW YORK

NOTE: The show will start prompt y at 8.00 P. M. due to the new Federal regulations that all places of amusement must close at 12:00 O'CLOCK.

Buy War Bonds !!

Admission	.80
Fed. Tax	.16
City Tax	.04
Total	$1.00

Image 16. Another example of varied events in the community to support the ward effort in early 1945 was the play and dance sponsored by La Fraternal, The oldest Spanish-speaking organization in Philadelphia at the time.

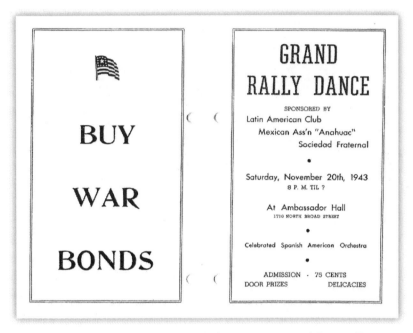

Image 17. During WW II, Puerto Ricans and other Latinos supported the war efforts with events to Buy War bonds. In 1943, three of the groups: La Fraternal, the Mexican Association Anahuac and the Latin American Club sponsored a big dance to collect funds for the war effort. At the time, future leader of the Puerto Rican community, Dr. Jose DeCelis was the president of the Latin American Club.

Image 18. Flyer by the Spanish Committee, a group of several organizations also sponsored events to support the war effort in 1945.

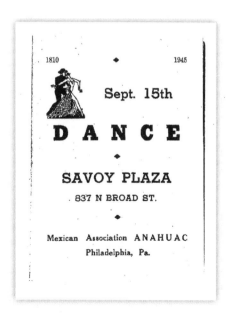

Image 19. Another celebration of Mexican Independence in 1945 shows the continued efforts stay connected to countries origin. These events always attracted Spanish-speakers from across the spectrum of city residents.

CHAPTER 5

The Emergence of a Puerto Rican Community: Social and Organizational Roots

Introduction

This chapter focuses on the early social and organizational roots of the Puerto Rican community building process in Philadelphia. This effort was considerably shaped by the continuous colonial relationship between the United States and Puerto Rico. Beginning in the early twentieth century, Puerto Ricans along with other Hispanics initiated a community development process that spanned the first four decades of the twentieth century. Before World War I, Puerto Ricans helped to found both a mutual aid society and a Spanish-language catholic chapel. Both of these institutions were originally located in Southwark (see maps). In the 1920s and 1930s, as the numbers of Puerto Ricans grew and became more religiously diverse, some of them also founded a Spanish-speaking Protestant Mission. The Mission was utilized not only for religious services but also became a social service agency providing assistance to them as well as organizing cultural affirmative activities. By the beginning of World War II, Puerto Rican and other Latino-based groups in Philadelphia were operating across enclave boundaries and sponsoring events that served to unite the different nationality and class groups into a Spanish-speaking colonia.

Initially, Puerto Ricans and other Latinos in Philadelphia began their community development process both within and between small enclaves, in which there was not a great deal of segregation. These ethnic enclaves, as will be discussed, were urban spaces shared with other ethnic and racial groups. During the interwar period, however, the network of connections among the three distinct Spanish-speaking enclaves of Southwark, Spring Garden and Northern Liberties cemented the community (see maps).[1]

The organizational network that sprang up within the Spanish-speaking enclaves of Philadelphia became, by the end of World War II, a rich cultural mosaic representing Puerto Ricans and other Spanish-speaking nationality groups in the city. Utilizing a combination of mutual aid, labor, social, cultural religious organizational formats, Philadelphia Puerto Ricans established the parameters for the appearance

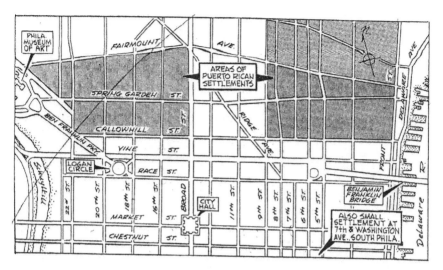

Map 2. This map reflects the influx of Puerto Ricans and the growth as well by the early 1950s. Note the reference to Puerto Ricans living in Southwark as well as the larger areas of Spring Garden and Northern Liberties.

of a community. It was this community, comprised significantly of Puerto Rican migrants, which served as a welcome mat for the large numbers of Puerto Ricans who arrived in Philadelphia after 1945. The network of religious, social and cultural groups that evolved between 1910 and 1945 formed the backbone of the Puerto Rican community that emerged in the 1950s and 1960s. The roots of the present-day Puerto Rican community in Philadelphia can be traced directly to the community building efforts of the pioneer groups in the interwar period.

The efforts to carve out several Spanish-speaking enclaves in Philadelphia were strengthened and enhanced by the arrival of Puerto Ricans. Newly arriving Puerto Ricans went to work alongside other Hispanics, frequented the same churches and joined their social organizations and, in some cases, helped to form new ones during the interwar period. The period between World War I and World War II was crucial to the consolidation of these enclaves into a vibrant Puerto Rican community evident by 1945. Consequently, by the time of the Great Migration or Wave of Puerto Ricans to the United States took off from the island (1945–1965), Philadelphia had become an increasingly significant point of attraction for these migrants because of this communal base.[2]

Support Organizations that facilitated the evolution
of a Puerto Rican Community

The three enclaves of Southwark, Spring Garden and Northern Liberties, developed organizations and leadership across the city, which helped to consolidate them into one colonia. Although many Spanish-speaking organizations contributed to the consolidation of the Puerto Rican colonia, four religious and social organizations had the greatest impact on the cohesion and consolidation of Puerto Ricans and other Latinos in Philadelphia between the early twentieth century and the end of World War II. These organizations were: Our Lady of the Miraculous Medal, La Milagrosa a Catholic Chapel, the Hispanic American Fraternal Association La Fraternal, the First Spanish Evangelical Mission and the International Institute.

Two of these institutions were founded in Southwark, within the oldest Latino enclave in the city. La Fraternal established in 1908 and La Milagrosa established in 1909 were founded within one year and two blocks from each other. Together these two organizations proved to be pivotal in the evolution of not only the Spanish-speaking enclave of Southwark, but of the other two enclaves as well. In the 1920s, the increasing numbers of Puerto Ricans and other Latinos in the city also developed a greater religious diversity. Spanish-speaking Protestants, though smaller in numbers than their Catholic brethren, began to organize their own church. Initially, inter-denominational in nature, Spanish-speaking Protestants eventually founded the First Spanish Evangelical Mission, in 1929. The fruits of this effort added another organizational layer to the Spanish-speaking enclaves of the city, especially for those residents of Spring Garden, where the Mission was first housed. When the Mission became the First Spanish Baptist Church in 1946, it moved to more permanent quarters in Northern Liberties, its facilities became an important community center for that enclave.

La Fraternal was formed as a mutual aid group. It came about as the result of a community meeting held during 1907. It is unclear exactly when and how this meeting was organized, but writing in 1910, Father Antonio Casulleras, the Parrish priest in charge of La Milagrosa indicated that the "gathering ... led to the formation of a ... well known society [La Fraternal]... for all Spanish-speaking people" (1910: 2). Increasingly, the group served as a social center celebrating annual events like El Dia de la Raza, (Day of the Race), Columbus Day and many other similar celebrations. The group used several different locations for its functions, but two: Boslover Hall and Garden Hall were located right in Southwark. The activities held at these different locations brought together Latinos from all parts of the city.

The headquarters of La Fraternal were located at 419 Pine Street in the heart of the Southwark Latino enclave. For Puerto Ricans and other Spanish-speaking residents of Southwark, the formation of La Fraternal, with its many evening events, plays, discussions, dances and festivals marked a turning point in the development of their communal emergence in the city. These affairs celebrated Hispanic identity of the many Latin American nationality groups. It also highlighted the universality of language (Spanish) and a sense of connection to the mother country (Spain). But, more importantly, the celebration of la Raza, allowed the diverse Spanish-speaking groups in the city to come together and share unitary elements of language, culture and family. The events organized by La Fraternal inevitably included a literary or cultural portion, usually in the form of a short performance (plays, vignettes, etc.). Keynote speakers were always included in the programs. Oftentimes the speakers represented the diverse Spanish-speaking consulates residing in Philadelphia at the time. Also, events usually ended with a dance party and celebration late into the night.

On the protestant side, what eventually became the First Spanish Baptist Church, as was earlier pointed out, started out in Spring Garden in 1929. According to Puerto Rican theologian and scholar, Edwin David Aponte, at that particular time, there appeared to be little intense religious partisanship among Latino Protestants in Philadelphia. The absence of bickering among Protestant Spanish-speakers, argues Aponte probably led to the formation of the Bible Study Group that first met in September 1929. Led by a student of the Philadelphia School of the Bible, William Strong this group evolved and began using space in the Fifth Baptist Church located at 18th and Spring Garden Streets. The group was made up of Puerto Rican, Cuban and Mexican families, some of whom had moved to Philadelphia during WW I. They met more or less regularly and in 1933, Oscar Rodriguez, a Puerto Rican, took up the ministerial duties of the group and leadership of the mission. Rodriguez was a student attending the Eastern Baptist Theological Seminary at the time; he pastored to Spanish-speakers in Philadelphia until the late 1930s (Aponte et al. 1994: 35–8; Koss 1965: 65).

The local International Institute was a fourth organizational entity that had a major impact on the consolidation and development of Latino groups in Philadelphia in the 1920s. The Institute, a part of a national network of groups initially started by local YWCAs in New York City, supported both cultural and ethnic pluralism while at the same time seeking... "a better integration of immigrants and their children in American society." The character of this support was different from what usually was found by groups in favor of the "Americanization" of foreigners in this time period. Beginning in the 1920s, the Philadelphia-based International Institute became interested in the local Spanish-speaking community (Mohl 1982: 37–41; Morton 1936).

The International Institutes were among those organizations, which served immigrants in the area of education and accommodation into the United States. The first Institute was founded in 1910 in Greenwich Village, New York a major immigrant district at the time. By the mid-1920s there were more than fifty-five similar institutes operating in the U.S., mostly in urban, immigrant-rich centers. The Institutes remained part of the YWCA until the 1930s when they severed connections and formed a national agency called the National Institute of Immigrant Welfare. According to historian Raymond A. Mohl (1982: 37), the International Institute of Philadelphia played a unique role in the city, as well as in Boston and San Francisco.

The International Institute emphasized its belief in cultural pluralism understood as a "federation of nationalities," where each group was supported by its own ethnic, religious and cultural affirmation. For Spanish-speakers in Philadelphia the cultural pluralistic view meant that, as an immigrant community, many of their social needs would be provided for at the Institute; including job search and even English classes. Parts of these services were meant to Americanize the immigrants, but while participating they could not only maintain their respective language and culture, but affirm them as well. The latter was accomplished by the formation of nationality based folklore groups. These cultural support efforts of the Philadelphia International Institute led to the creation of dance and other cultural groups. Two in particular were the Mexican group, Anahuac and a Puerto Rican group called the Club Juventud Hispana; others representing Cuba, Spain and Venezuela were also organized. Once a year, during the month of May, these groups came together and held a Folk Festival at the Institute (Mohl 1982: 39; Morton 1936).

These four organizations, among others served to bring together individuals and families across class and ethnic lines. The leadership of La Fraternal was most reflective of the diversity of the enclaves. Mostly led by Spaniards or persons of Spanish descent, the leadership group tended to be made up mostly of professionals or small shop owners from the different enclaves. Yet, their events seemed to gather persons of all classes including cigar makers. By the later 1930s and early 1940s, La Fraternal's leadership passed into the hands of Cuban *tampeños* and Puerto Ricans, a reflection of the increase of these two groups in the city. A key feature of the leadership of La Fraternal throughout this period was that it included people who lived in the three enclaves of Spring Garden, Northern Liberties and Southwark. This last point is significant because it implies the interconnection among the respective enclaves.

La Milagrosa was always thoroughly diverse. Its membership lists, baptism and marriage records, as well as its social affairs all reflect a diverse sampling of the different Spanish-speaking groups that made up the colonia. The same holds true for the First Spanish Evangelical Mission, although during World War II, because of the pastoral work of Rev. Enrique Rodriguez (no relations to Oscar Rodriguez) among Puerto Rican contract laborers, the institution reflected a higher blue-collar membership than either La Fraternal or La Milagrosa. As for the International Institute, its doors were opened to all Latinos but, they tended to work more directly with each nationality group and offered their services (English classes, etc.) across class lines. Together, these four institutions portray a highly active, culturally rich and divergent groups working in cooperation to meet the diverse need of Puerto Ricans and other Latinos in the city. Just how these different organizations and enclaves intersected with other dimensions of community life can be gleaned from a synopsis of the activities of each one of them.

Each settlement, Southwark, Spring Garden and Northern Liberties developed around the social networks and businesses in each area. However, the institutions discussed above served to further the interests of Puerto Ricans and other Latinos, in all aspects of the formation and development of a Spanish-speaking colonia. It is important to note that although these enclaves were separated by some distance, the four institutions helped to bring together residents from each one in an intersection of class and ethnicity. It was this interconnection that led to further migration and concentration of Puerto Rican migrants into a colonia that provided for linguistic and cultural unity.

In the 1920s, when Luis Alvarez, a Puerto Rican arrived in Philadelphia he established a grocery store on South 3rd and Bainbridge streets. In addition, he sold fresh produce in the Head House market located at 2nd Street. At the time, Spaniards predominantly made up the Spanish-speaking population of Southwark. In the period between 1920 and 1940, the enclave of Southwark evolved into a predominantly Puerto Rican area. Expanding from the area around South 4th and Pine Streets, the area incorporated bordered by Pine Street on the north, 11th street on the east, Spruce Street on the south and 13th Street on the west. The Southwark colonia also expanded to include an area bounded by Chestnut and Fitzwater streets on the north and south, Broad and Front streets on the west and east.

For Latinos in Southwark, Boslover Hall, located at 7th and Pine streets had become an important dance hall and social gathering place for Spanish-speakers across Philadelphia since the late 1920s. The Head House Market, which ran the length of S. 2nd Street, between Lombard and South streets, was a significant business sector for Latinos in Southwark. The market not only provided fresh produce, including products from Spanish-speaking countries but was also a source of income for those, who like Luis Alvarez, Sr., owned and operated a kiosk on location (Alvarez 2000).[3]

The Latino congregation that met in 1908 in Southwark realized that they needed spiritual as well as social organizations that could lead to greater benefit and success. This group, which included Puerto Ricans, Spaniards, Cubans, Mexicans, and other Central and South Americans, strove for this goal. The creation of the Mission of the Miraculous Medal in 1909 in the basement of St. Mary's Catholic Church in Southwark was a very important step.

Marriage and baptism records for those first years reflect that cigar makers also fared prominently amongst the early parishioners of La Milagrosa. As the Mission set up ongoing operations in the basement of the schoolhouse located next to the historic Church of St. Mary's, the Mission of La Milagrosa continued to serve the spiritual needs of this population for its first three years of existence (1909–1912). It was evident early on that the allotted space was insufficient for all the parishioners that traveled from many parts of the City to marry and baptize their children in the church. It was at this time that representatives of the Spanish-speaking community asked the Philadelphia Archdiocese for assistance in securing permanent quarters for the Mission. In 1912, permanent quarters were acquired in Spring Garden where it existed for more than 100 years (Casulleras 1910: 1; Rickle 1996: 40; *Philadelphia Evening Bulletin* 1912).

The initial presence of La Milagrosa in Southwark contributed to the consolidation of this ethnic enclave. For three years, 1909–1912, La Milagrosa provided religious services, in Spanish to the local population. Although the Mission did not cater exclusively to Latinos in Southwark, many of those who married and/or baptized their children in those early years were, in fact, residents of the neighborhood.

Aside from the regular social events held at Boslover Hall, many Spanish-speaking men found it very difficult to frequent the bars in the neighborhood. In Southwark, Latino men could purchase beer through back doors of establishments but could not sit down in the bar because many of them, due to whatever particular skin tone they possessed, were often treated the same as blacks and had to make their purchases through a back door or window. This led to the establishment of a number of speakeasies that catered to Spanish-speakers. One such place was owned and operated by a Puerto Rican woman, Carmen Ferrer who used an apartment on South Street for this purpose. Ferrer had come from Puerto Rico and worked as a cook for Puerto Rican migrant workers on farms in southern New Jersey. She initially settled in Spring Garden, but moved to Southwark and established a business in the neighborhood (Santiago 1994).

While the Southwark enclave developed around the cigar making shops, the piers and the economic activity along South Street, the Spring Garden enclave also grew and expanded during the period from 1920 to 1940. The enclave was then bounded by Poplar and Vine streets on the north and south, and 23rd and Broad streets, on the west and east. For many Latinos, the allure of jobs, especially at the giant Baldwin Locomotive Works was reason enough to live in Spring Garden. But, one of the most important reasons why Spring Garden attracted so many Puerto Ricans in this time period had to do with the move of La Milagrosa to the heart of this enclave. Once La Milagrosa moved from Southwark to permanent quarters in Spring Garden in 1912, its location at 1903 Spring Garden Street, the chapel's facilities began to expand beyond religious services to include charity work as well.

By the mid-1920s', La Milagrosa had developed into a hub of activity for the community. The chapel organized an Association of La Milagrosa, which handled many of the social aspects of the services provided. The Association was responsible for organizing classes in English, recreational activities and picnics among others. By the end of the decade the chapel had become an important institutional center. The additional acquisition of a property located at 1836 Brandywine Street, around the corner from La Milagrosa, which became known as the Spanish Catholic Club (see photos of confirmation), helped the chapel expand its facilities. This location was used primarily for social functions such as dances. However, the facility was also rented out for weddings and baptism parties. Social functions at the Club attracted many Latinos from the other enclaves as well. La Milagrosa also organized a Youth Club, which was co-sponsored by the International Institute and functioned right in the neighborhood (*Polk's Philadelphia City Directory* 1935–36: 2004; Bermudez 1999).

The physical presence of the International Institute in Spring Garden also attracted many Spanish-speakers to the area. Located at 635 N. 15th Street, near Mount Vernon, the Institute's location was within four blocks of La Milagrosa. The broad range of services provided by the Institute's social workers to immigrants, especially to Spaniards, Cubans, Mexicans and Venezuelans also added to the organization's attraction for Spanish-speakers in the vicinity. The initial efforts to establish a Protestant Spanish-language church in the neighborhood also contributed to the expansion of the Spring Garden enclave (Aponte et al. 1994: 38: Koss 1965: 65).

Before the First Spanish Evangelical Mission moved to Northern Liberties, this area had been a hub of Spanish-speaking activity: it expanded in the late 1930s and early 1940s. By that time, Vine and Masters Streets bounded the enclave on the South and North, Broad and Front streets on the west and east. There were several key features that led to the expansion of Puerto Ricans and Latinos in Northern Liberties. One of them was that there were many cigar-making factories in the area. In fact, the Cigar Makers International Union Local #165, the main labor organization of cigar makers, at the time had its offices located at 1334 Spring Garden Street. In the early 1930s, the Bayuk Brothers Cigar Company opened another factory at 9th Street and Columbia Avenue in North Philadelphia. This fact attracted many cigar makers, men and women to the Northern Liberties area. Antonio Malpica, who owned his own "chinchal" (small cigar making shop) also free-lanced at some of the cigar factories.

One of those cigar-making "chinchales" was owned and operated by a Latino known as "El Jefe", the Chief. His cigar making shop was located on Marshall Street near Brown, in the heart of Northern Liberties (Canales 1999; Bermudez 1999).

One of the main reasons why the area attracted so many Latinos was the Marshall Street market (see photos). Between 1920 and 1960, the stretch of Marshall Street running north from Spring Garden Street to Girard Avenue was a hub of commercial activity that attracted many Spanish-speaking workers. The many Jewish-owned shops resembled the Orchard Street area of the Lower Eastside of Manhattan. Just like in New York, the area attracted Spanish-speakers to work in the nearby cigar factories, garment factories, and consequently to live in the neighborhood. The core area of present-day Spanish-speaking Philadelphia is still physically connected to the Marshall Street hub.[4]

The area surrounding the Marshall Street Market was a hub of activity; it was the northern equivalent of the Italian Market located on Ninth Street, in South Philadelphia. Consequently, Marshall Street attracted many Spanish-speakers because, not only could they find many of the products they liked, including fresh meat and live poultry but many of them found jobs with the Jewish merchants established in the area. Socially, the Marshall Street area included a number of dance halls and movie theaters. The most prominent location for events sponsored by Spanish-speaking groups was the Pannonia Hall, located on Franklin Street, near Fairmount Avenue. For instance, Domingo Martinez got his start in a grocery business working for a Spaniard who owned a store on Marshall Street.

Under the leadership Reverend Enrique Rodriguez, the First Spanish Evangelical Mission became an important religious as well as community center in its new location. So pivotal was this move to this particular neighborhood, that Puerto Ricans were not only attracted there, but also branched out moving north into the heart of North Philadelphia in the ensuing decades. Reverend Rodriguez frequently preached to Puerto Rican migrant workers in New Jersey's farms and to industrial workers like the Campbell Soup Company located just across the river from Philadelphia, in their respective barracks. Many of these workers searched out Reverend Rodriguez once their contracts were expired and moved to Philadelphia to the neighborhood where his church stood. These new members of the Spanish Baptist Mission, once established in Philadelphia, oftentimes sent for their respective families, thus contributing to the expansion of the colonia (Aponte et al. 1994: 38; Koss 1965: 65).

Like many other immigrants in Philadelphia, especially those of the Catholic faith, Puerto Ricans tended to live near churches that met their spiritual needs. In 1912, La Milagrosa Mission moved from its Southwark location to a building located at 1903 Spring Garden Street, in the heart of that Spanish-speaking hub.

The chapel quickly became a form of community as well as spiritual center. But, most importantly, La Milagrosa served the community by providing for baptisms and weddings, as indicated by the parish's baptismal and wedding records for those years. The records document the incipient networks of godparents and friends, many of whom lived within walking distance from the church. Indeed, the largest portion, about a third of all those married and/or baptized in the chapel during this time period resided in Spring Garden. In addition, many Spanish-speakers from Southwark and other parts of Philadelphia continued to attend church at the new location (Archdiocese of Philadelphia 1910–45).[5]

Institutional and Community Development

By the early1940s, a Puerto Rican community had begun to take shape in Philadelphia. An affirmation of ethnic and religious belief contributed to consolidating the links between the enclaves. Churches, as well as the International Institute and the Hispanic Fraternal Association better known as La Fraternal were the strongest institutionally, and also, had the greatest long-term impact on the evolving community. These institutions reflected change over time in the evolution of Puerto Ricans in the city.

Language, culture and an increasing organizational network characterized three Hispanic enclaves. The consolidation of the community was particularly helped by the work of La Fraternal in Southwark, La Milagrosa in Spring Garden, the First Spanish Baptist Mission, as well as the community-wide work of the International Institute. Each one of these entities contributed to the inter-community relationships among Latinos in Philadelphia during the 1930s and 1940s. During World War II, these groups, along with others founded in that period, came together to foster their language and cultural presence in the city as well as to support the war effort. By their actions, Puerto Ricans and other Latinos in the City during the war began to claim a wider audience citywide. The efforts of these residents solidified their community and positioned it for further development, which occurred, in the ensuing decades of the second half of the twentieth century (see photos).

The aforementioned organizations also fostered the institutional fortification of the Spanish-speaking enclaves into a community. Along with other organizational efforts and led by a wide group of religious leaders and professionals, these organizations sponsored a series of linguistic and cultural events such as dances, beauty pageants and the like, which affirmed their ethnicity and religious beliefs.

In particular, La Milagrosa sponsored the formation of La Milagrosa Association, a lay group of members of the church. The Association was responsible for organizing the church's social and charitable events. The Association was formed around the time of World War I. Although, during the first few years of the decade membership in the Association of La Milagrosa dropped, by 1925 it began to pick up again. The losses in membership during the 1922–24 periods may be a reflection of the post-war depression and the return to Spain of a large number of nationals. The fact remains that this Association grew dramatically after 1925. In part, the renewed activism was due to new, young priests who came to serve at the Chapel at that time. Prominent amongst the chapel's new leadership was Father Antonio Capdevilla, who remained involved with the chapel well into the late 1950's (see photos). Amongst the initiatives of La Milagrosa was the physical expansion of the church from 150 to 220 seats, this allowed for an increase in the number of masses on Sundays. In addition, Father Juan Sastre, another of the new priests, organized a Women's Auxiliary, the Daughters of Mary, to whom Mary Rodriguez belonged, while Father Capdevilla formed the Hispanic Youth Group. This group became a cornerstone of the community and brought together the second generation headed by Puerto Ricans like Antonio Arroyo in many recreational events; the group lasted well into the 1940's. Also, religious instruction increased during this period when in 1926, a group of Trinitarian nuns established five different groups of students for this purpose.

In the 1930s, the chapel acquired another property, about a block and a half away, which it turned into a hall used for social functions. The Spanish Catholic Club, as it was known, was located at 1836 Brandywine Street in Spring Garden. The Hall attracted Latino patrons from all of the enclaves and was also available for renting for weddings and baptism events. Meanwhile, those of the Catholic faith continued to attend mass, marry in La Milagrosa, and baptize their children. By the mid-1930s, the chapel was organizing increasing numbers of events and the membership of the Association continued to grow. A record high of 52 confirmations were administered in one year alone and the Hispanic Youth group continued to be very active (Archdiocese of Philadelphia 1910–45).

On the cultural front, the Spanish-born priests who served in the Chapel helped emphasize the Hispanicity of the community through spiritual and social events conducted in Spanish. The fact that the Order of Vincentian, based in Barcelona, Spain provided the personnel for the chapel contributed to the ethnic identity of the community. These priests generally encouraged immigrants to form associations, establish newspapers, and often helped to settle clashes between employers and employees, as well as with different immigrant groups.

The International Institute continued in its support of Pan-Hispanic groups throughout the 1930s and 1940s. For instance, the Institute sponsored the Mexican Association Anahuac which continued functioning in this period and, still exists even today. Even when Spanish-speaking groups discontinued, the Institute continued to invite former members, like those of the Club Juventud Hispana, to its events (see fliers). In 1939, the Juventud Hispana was reorganized by the youth of La Milagrosa; they continued to meet until 1942, when some of the most active members married and moved away. The relationship between the Institute and other more established Spanish-speaking organizations, like La Fraternal, also were sustained all throughout this period (Fereshetian 1951; Sánchez Korrol 1994: 18–9; Centro de Estudios Puertorriqueños 1982: 4–4).

The work of the International Institute of Philadelphia was noted even in Puerto Rico. In 1946, Clarence Senior, American sociologist and Research Director of the Social Science Research Center of the University of Puerto Rico and soon-to-be appointed head of the U.S.-based Puerto Rican Migration Division Office in New York, wrote to the International Institute of Philadelphia. In his letter to Marion Lantz, Director of the Institute, Senior inquired about the local Puerto Rican community. At the time, Senior was preparing a manuscript on the Puerto Rican migration experience, a study that was published later that year. Senior's interest, however, also denotes the Institute's prestige as an agency that served immigrants in the city, especially Puerto Ricans and who amassed reliable data on these groups (Moreno 1945; Senior 1946).[6]

The belief of the Institute in cultural pluralism allowed immigrant groups to retain their respective ethnic characteristics through folklore and other means, this helped Puerto Ricans assert their national pride while at the same time receiving support from the agency in learning the English language and other American cultural mores needed for survival in a strange environment. The end result of the Institute's early work with Latinos in Philadelphia was their contribution to organizational and institutional development of these enclaves. Also, when Puerto Ricans began arriving in Philadelphia in greater numbers after World War II, the International Institute, later known as the Nationalities Services Center, became one of the primary agencies supporting the new migrants in acclimating to the United States.[7]

When the Reverend Enrique Rodriguez came to Philadelphia during WW II, he brought with him the pastoral experience he had garnered in Coamo, Puerto Rico. Reverend Rodriguez also brought with him pastoral experience from his work in a military plant in Connecticut. This particular experience invariably helped him in preaching to Puerto Rican laborers at the Campbell Soup Company in Camden and migrant farm workers in southern New Jersey, generally. Rodriguez also assisted contracted laborers to move from those farms to settle in the city of Philadelphia. Many of those workers followed their minister to Spring Garden, where Rodriguez and his wife Ramonita had settled (Aponte et al. 1994: 35; Koss 1965: 65).

In addition to the groups already discussed (La Milagrosa, La Fraternal, the International Institute and the First Spanish Evangelical Mission) there were a few other smaller ones whose organizational efforts played a part in the consolidation of the Puerto Rican community during World War II. One of these endeavors was the establishment of the Misión Evangélica/Fifth Street Community Center at 551–553 N. 5th Street by the Reverend Ralph Cárdenas. Cardenas, a Spaniard, had come to Philadelphia to study at the Baptist Seminar; he graduated in 1926. Along with his Puerto Rican wife, Lucrecia, Cardenas ran the church and a center. Cardenas was a full time minister; he helped the Church's members with legal problems, finding employment or securing Home Relief (public assistance).

The Friends Neighborhood Guild (FNG) was another organization that helped Puerto Ricans during and after the Second World War. The Guild, a settlement house established in 1890, was located at 4th and Green Streets, at the time in the heart of the Northern Liberties enclave. The FNG provided space for Puerto Ricans to gather and socialize. The Guild also provided space for city resources and services, like the Health Department to be brought in to serve the Puerto Rican population in the area. These two institutions also made their mark in helping cement the basis of Puerto Rican Philadelphia in this time period (Santiago 1999; Koss 1965: 70; Whalen 1994: 400).[8]

The religious and social services of La Milagrosa, La Fraternal, the International Institute, and the First Spanish Evangelical Mission and to a lesser extent the Misión Evangélica and Friends Neighborhood Guild, supported the buildup of these institutions as bastions of linguistic and cultural affirmation for Puerto Ricans and other Latinos in Philadelphia in the World War II period. Their efforts also helped these residents transform the Spanish-speaking enclaves of Southwark, Spring Garden and Northern Liberties into an intricate pattern of cross-neighborhood relationships. This network built a solid community.

A Leadership Emerges

The emergence of a local, committed and Spanish-speaking leadership in Philadelphia helped to shape these enclaves into a community. Clergymen, doctors, dentists, teachers, businessmen, bodegueros and other professionals surfaced to assume leadership in the community. Much like the eastern and southern European ethnic communities in Philadelphia, community leadership in the Spanish-speaking enclaves came mostly from the white-collar sectors or the small business community. It was a very similar process as the Polish community, as historian Caroline Golab has pointed out. Like the Polish community in Philadelphia, it was mostly the small store owners and white-collar workers, who could afford to live in one place for a prolonged period of time, generally surfaced as community leaders. Unskilled and semi-skilled workers, for the most part, tended to be more mobile, always in search of a job or better economic opportunities, and too unstable to provide the leadership needed to surpass in this process.

Dr. José DeCelis was one example of a Puerto Rican professional who lived in Spring Garden, in the same house for almost fifty years and for a good many of those years was a community leader. Antonio Arroyo, an early leader in the Hispanic Youth Formation, was a clerk. Domingo Martinez, a later leader, was the owner of a grocery store. Although, as pointed out earlier, semi-skilled and unskilled workers did not generally become community leaders, there were exceptions. One such exception was Frank Aday, originally from Tampa, Florida and who had been brought by his family to Philadelphia in the 1920's, worked as a counterman at a local diner. In the 1950s, Aday became a Democratic Party committeeman in the 15th ward (Spring Garden). It is interesting to point out that a number of these individuals were also active members of their respective churches. Women also played leadership roles, as exemplified by Aurora Alvarez, a schoolteacher and Amparo Sariego, who was Vice President of the Club Juventud Hispana and would later distinguish herself for providing support to the Spanish Republican cause (*Philadelphia Evening Bulletin* 1961).

It was, however, Dr. DeCelis who became the most prominent leader in this time period. In that early period, Dr. DeCelis was also an active member of La Milagrosa. In addition, he was President of the Latin American Club, one of the most active groups in the colonia during World War II. For more than forty-two years, DeCelis dedicated himself to his profession as a dentist. He also devoted much of his time working to improve the lives of those who lived in his neighborhood (*Philadelphia Sunday Bulletin* 1958).

World War II: Organizational Activities among Latinos and Wartime Labor Assist a Community to Take Shape

World War II was a defining period in the evolution of the Puerto Rican community in Philadelphia. Two meaningful components of this development were (1)- the notable increase in social activity of the various Pan-Hispanic organizations in the city during this time, and (2) a significant increase of the Puerto Rican population in the city, particularly made up of migrant wartime workers. There was a marked expansion in the social activities among Spanish-speaking groups during the war years as can be gleaned from flyers and other promotional materials utilized for these events. One interesting feature of these materials is that they were produced in English, probably to attract a wider audience beyond the enclaves, as well as some second-generation migrants who may have used English increasingly as their primary means of communication. The use of English and American war symbols was also intended to appease the larger Philadelphia society much like the immigrant patriotic rallies that were organized in Philadelphia during the First World War. It is also noteworthy that events sponsored by Spanish-speaking organizations during the war years invariably promoted and sold war bonds. The sale of war bonds furthermore, denotes a degree of patriotism for the new land on the part of Latinos, a sense of belonging and cooperation.

Puerto Rican migration to the United States increased dramatically during World War II. Despite limitations in transportation facilities during the war, the numbers of Puerto Rican migrants increased in each fiscal year between 1941-42 and 1945-46. Evidently, military service accounted for some of the growth, but it was wartime employment, which, together with economic hardships already existent on the island, fueled emigration in this period. During 1943 and 1944 specifically, the inclusion of Puerto Ricans in the labor recruitment efforts of the War Manpower Commission accounted for the migration of thousands of island laborers to the Philadelphia region. A great many of these wartime laborers found their way to the increasingly notable Puerto Rican community in the city. Some of the laborers were drawn to the city by the by ministerial work of the Reverend Enrique Rodriguez pastor of the First Spanish Evangelical Mission as well as the outreach of many diverse cultural and social organizations. This made the influx of Puerto Rican migrants during the war all the more impressive. This effort became a precursor to the labor recruitment efforts of the immediate postwar period.[9]

The location at which events were held during the war included not only those spots within the Spanish-speaking enclaves like the Boslover Hall located at 7th and Pine streets and the Musical Fund Hall located at 8th and Locust streets in Southwark but, also locations outside of the community like the "Grand Rally Dance" held in 1943 at the Ambassador Hall, located 1701 North Broad Street. This event is illustrative of the period for several reasons. First, the event was promoted as a "United War Chest Rally" and was sponsored by the "Spanish Committee." (See Promotional Program in Appendix). Highlighted in the program were the American flag and, in large bold letters the words "Buy War Bonds." Clearly, events such as these reflected not only the coming together of members of the different Latino groups, an important accomplishment in its own, but of greater significance was the establishment of the colonia as a part of the larger Philadelphia community. Undoubtedly, the American war symbols were not lost on those outside of the community who attended the event or who saw the promotional materials for the same.

The range of events held by the different Latino groups in the 1940s spanned from the cultural, affirming national holidays like the Commemoration of Mexican

Independence or the political like the dance sponsored by the International Workers Order. By and large, the bulk of social events organized by Latino groups in Philadelphia during this time provided a theater and dance in Spanish. Despite the emphasis on the war themes (the sale of war bonds, for instance) at these events, the main purpose was to bring together the different groups and to be entertained by musicians reflecting the specter of the Spanish-speaking migrant world residing in the United States. Events such as the "Queen Festival" held in June 1941, at the Ambassador Hall, were more typical of these gatherings. This event co-sponsored by La Fraternal, the Mexican Association Anahuac and the Latin American Club held a beauty pageant. It may have been the first of its kind in Philadelphia. The festival featured three contestants, one representing each of the groups. The main speakers on the program at this event also reflected the diversity of the community. One of the main speakers that night was Professor Octavio Diaz Valenzuela, who lived just a few short blocks away from the Hall located on Broad Street and Montgomery Avenue. Diaz Valenzuela taught Spanish at Temple University and also served as Vice Consul for Colombia. Ms. Irene Zarraga, who won the beauty contest that night, was the daughter of Tomás and Maria Zarraga. The Zarragas were Spaniards who lived on Palmer Street in the Fishtown river ward section of the city. The Master of Ceremonies at the event was Juan Mulet, a Cuban who owned a grocery store located on Pine Street in Southwark. The multi-national diversity of this gathering is indicative that while Latinos in Philadelphia lived in several areas of the city, events such as this one could bring them all together in one night and presumably for other purposes as well (Senior 1947: 8; *Philadelphia City Directory* 1935–36: 171).

Increasingly, these types of mutually sponsored events led to a greater connection and camaraderie among the groups throughout this period. These three groups: La Fraternal, Latin American Club and Club Anahuac represented the diversity of the Spanish-speaking colonia in Philadelphia during the Second World War. The offices of La Fraternal, during the war continued to be located at 419 Pine Street in the heart of Latino Southwark, while the president of the organization, Santiago Feigor resided at 5331 Addison Street in West Philadelphia. Club Anahuac, a group organized under the auspices of the International Institute was made up of Mexicans. While its headquarters were located at the Institutes' building in Spring Garden, its president, Pedro Alvarez lived on Ogontz Avenue in the Oak Lane section of Philadelphia. It is not clear where the offices of the Latin American Club were, if it had any, but this group seems to have been the most diverse. Its membership included Puerto Ricans, Mexicans, Spaniards, and Cubans. In 1941, the president of the Latin American Club was Julio Noval, a clerk who lived at 3301 Spring Garden Street, right across the Schuylkill River from the Spring Garden enclave (*La Prensa* 1941: 8; *Philadelphia City Directory* 1935–36: 744).

The use of theatrical and musical groups based in New York also contributed to solidifying a regional relationship between the two cities, already evident since the 1920s, when the Spanish language daily newspaper, *La Prensa*, based in New York City began to carry news about events in the Pan-Hispanic enclaves of Philadelphia. New York and Philadelphia were connected in several ways that are important for the relationship between the Spanish-speaking colonias in both cities. Commercially, ships that traveled between New York and the Caribbean also made stops in Philadelphia. In addition, Philadelphia was an important stop for ground transportation in the northeast corridor between Boston and Washington, D.C. It was relatively easy to travel by rail between Philadelphia and New York. The connection between both cities was also cemented by the numerous reports in *La Prensa* during the interwar period. By the early 1950s, this newspaper had established a regular column entitled: *En Filadelfia* which was written by Philadelphia Puerto Rican community leader, Domingo Martinez (Rodriguez 1999; Canales 1999).[10]

World War II had a distinct impact on the growth of Puerto Ricans in Philadelphia. Labor recruitment efforts during the war continued in the postwar period thus attracting thousands more migrants to Pennsylvania and New Jersey. Although at the height of the Great Depression in the 1930s, unemployment in the U.S. had reached 25% by 1942, with the country at war, millions of men in the Armed Services and the Defense Industry operating at full throttle, a labor shortage developed. This was especially true in the Philadelphia region where the Campbell Soup Company, the Hurff Canning Company, the Baltimore-Ohio Railroad Company and Baldwin Locomotives Company as well as farms in Southern New Jersey and Eastern Pennsylvania, especially during the harvest season, found themselves in need of recruiting more workers. Some of these industries like the Campbell Soup company were contracted by the federal government to provide canned goods for soldiers fighting overseas. One of those agencies, the War Manpower Commission (WMC), was charged with soliciting and distributing labor for defense industries. The WMC was initially reluctant to hire Puerto Ricans. Reviewing the case of the WMC, historian Carmen Teresa Whalen found that the previous experiences of hiring Puerto Ricans to do farm work had confronted problems when, after short periods of time, these workers left the farms for better paying jobs in the City. Compounding this issue was the fact that as U.S. citizens, Puerto Ricans could not be deported once their labor contracts expired. But, pressure from U.S. congressmen from States suffering labor shortages and administration officials on the Island prevailed to include Puerto Ricans as contract laborers for defense work (Whalen 2001: 49–52).

As local papers and even the company itself indicated, by late 1943 and early 1944, Campbell Soup was short of workers in their canning operations in Camden, New Jersey. In early 1944, the business community through its *Business Week* magazine reported that arrangements had been made to recruit Puerto Rican laborers despite earlier resistance to do so. In its April 22, 1944 issue, *Business Week* reported that the railroads eyed with "mixed ambitions" the decision to recruit 2000 Puerto Ricans for unskilled jobs on their lines. The year before these rail road companies had imported Mexicans, Bahamians and Puerto Rican workers with mixed results; some Puerto Ricans had walked off the jobs. A week later, however, *Business Week* announced that at least three major industries were readying to hire 3000 Puerto Ricans workers. The Baltimore-Ohio (B&O) Railroad Company planned to hire 2000 of them for disbursement throughout the Midwest and Campbell Soup and the Edgar F. Hurff canning Company would hire the other 1000. Thus began, auspiciously, what would become the largest labor contract program in Puerto Rico, with the blessings of Washington and the government of the Island (*Business Week* 1944a, 1944b). Several scholars of the Puerto Rican migration experience like Edwin Maldonado, Carmen Whalen and Jorge Duany have written extensively about this labor program, so this chapter will not go into many details. Suffice to say that the WW II labor recruitment and later the labor contract program contributed significantly to bringing Puerto Ricans to the Philadelphia region, many settling in the City in the 1940s and 1950s.

Utilizing the experience of the WMC in recruiting workers from Puerto Rico, Samuel Freedman, a Puerto Rican of German-American descent, who was also a farmer, began a transportation company to recruit farm workers from the Island to work in the US at the end of World War II. He hired two old Air Force planes, called the company Wings Caribe Airline, and flew recruits into the Northeast Philadelphia Airport. He used a friend in Puerto Rico to recruit contract laborers on the Island and paid the recruiters $25 per head. Freedman's contribution to bringing thousands of Puerto Rican laborers to the Philadelphia region has not been fully studied, his relationship with individuals in the Puerto Rican colonia in Philadelphia like the Reverend Enrique Rodriguez helped him channel many Puerto Ricans to the Spanish Baptist church in the immediate postwar years (Koss 1965: 66; Giusti 1975: 1). Rodriguez was instrumental in helping Puerto Rican migrant workers from the war industries and farms to relocate to Philadelphia. He would minister to the Puerto Rican Campbell Soup workers in their barracks on Sundays, and when many of them decided to move to Philadelphia, he helped them settle in around 16th Street and Fairmount where other Puerto Ricans lived (Koss 1965: 64–5).

In addition, Puerto Rican labor migrants, who came to work in the Philadelphia area during World War II, found the socio-linguistic and religious ambiance of the city a welcome relief to the doldrums of barracks-style living of South Jersey farms or the Campbell Soup factory. Labor shortages in the United States had brought thousands of Puerto Ricans to the area, but a lack of social and cultural activities could not keep them on the farm or the factory. Also, labor conditions, including meager, plain living quarters, unfamiliar food and a lack of Spanish-speaking personnel were often cited as reasons for Puerto Ricans to leave their employment on South Jersey farms and move to Philadelphia. Some Puerto Ricans returned to the island when their contracts expired but many more came following the "ambiente" in Philadelphia. A few Puerto Ricans like Marcelino Benitez not only kept their jobs at places like Campbell Soup but also made them careers.[11]

Towards the end of World War II, individuals like Puerto Rican-born Samuel Freedman capitalized on the labor shortage situation, especially on the farms of New Jersey, to establish a company of labor recruitment on the island. His knowledge of the language and customs, as well as his relationship with the growers in the New Jersey region placed him a unique situation to promote this endeavor. His contribution to bringing thousands more Puerto Rican laborers to the Philadelphia region and his relationship with the Reverend Enrique Rodriguez helped him channel many Puerto Ricans to his church in the immediate post-war years. Freedman's organizing efforts also led to the establishment of a Division of the Puerto Rican Migration Office in Glassboro, New Jersey in the late 1940s ascribed to the island's Department of Labor. Eventually, this office was moved to Philadelphia and became a cornerstone of social services to Puerto Rican migrants and their families.

Conclusion

By 1945, there existed a Puerto Rican community in Philadelphia. This greater community was evident for its Spanish-speaking settlement density and display of social identity denoted by its organizational output and regularity of activity. It had become a complex web of social, cultural and religious fervor.

For Mary Rodriguez, who had resided in the city since 1931 and had spent the war years traveling between her home and her job as a Post Office mail censor in New York, the Puerto Rican community had grown immensely. By 1945, in Spring Garden, the social and religious impact of La Milagrosa, where Mary Rodriguez was a lay nun, her husband Tomás, and their three children, worshipped, had turned the chapel into an important community center. On the other side of Broad Street, Antonio Malpica's boarding house and cigar-making shop was full of Puerto Rican laborers from the Campbell Soup Company as well as of merchant marines. Malpica's place was, more importantly, a social gathering locale, which, on occasion, also doubled as a watering hole. In addition, because Malpica was also a guitar player and his boarder Juan Canales, who also played guitar, had connections with other Puerto Rican and Cuban musicians based in New York, Malpica's place was always an attraction for visiting Latin musicians. On more than a few occasions his place was the center for many jam sessions; a real happening in the Northern Liberties enclave (Canales 1999; Rodriguez 1999).

Between the time Father Antonio Canas, who established the first mission of La Milagrosa in 1909 and the end of World War II, Puerto Ricans in Philadelphia had not only survived but also developed a solid base. Had he been alive in 1945, Father Canas would have been pleased and satisfied to see how the Spanish-speaking population especially Puerto Ricans had grown since those early days of La Milagrosa. For Dr. DeCelis, who did survive to witness the transformation, it must have made quite an impression. In 1945, DeCelis marked his thirtieth year in Philadelphia. He still lived in the same house at 862 N. 20th Street in the Spring Garden area. He had participated in many community events, had married and baptized two sons in La Milagrosa and had presided over the Latin American Club. Little did he imagine, as a young dental student, that he would live to see the birth and development of a Puerto Rican community in Philadelphia.

The arrival of Puerto Ricans in the first decades of the twentieth century enhanced the efforts of Pan-Hispanics in developing a significant organizational network of mutual aid, labor; and interconnected enclaves. Cultural identity and institutional development characterized the formation of a Puerto Rican community in Philadelphia by 1945. The intricate organizational network and leadership of this group played a decisive role in the development of the Puerto Rican community in the city during the 1950s and 1960s (Hernández Álvarez 1968: 41).

CHAPTER 6

Legacies for the Great Migration and Beyond: An Epilogue

Introduction

The small but significant organizational network that sprang up within the Spanish-speaking enclaves of Philadelphia became, by the end of World War II, a rich cultural mosaic representing Puerto Rican and other Spanish-speaking national groups in the city. Using a combination of mutual aid, labor, social, and cultural organizational formats, Philadelphia Puerto Ricans and other Latinos established the parameters for the appearance of a colonia. This colonia of Puerto Ricans and other Latinos served as a welcome mat for the large numbers of Puerto Ricans who arrived in Philadelphia after 1945. The network of religious, social, and cultural groups that evolved between 1910 and 1945 formed the backbone of the Puerto Rican community that existed in the 1950s and 1960s. The roots of the present-day Puerto Rican community in Philadelphia can be traced directly to the community-building efforts of the pioneer groups in the interwar period. This history has now begun to be told.

Along with the efforts of men like Samuel Freedman and the Reverend Enrique Rodriguez, the Puerto Rican colonia in Philadelphia grew exponentially during and immediately after World War II. By 1950, the basic outline of a distinct Puerto Rican community had begun to emerge. For Puerto Ricans, like long-term residents of Spring Garden Dr. Jose DeCelis, Mary Rodriguez and the Rev. Enrique Rodriguez, among others, the population increase was palpable as their compatriots moved in. In the case of Antonio Malpica, the Rev. Ralph Cardenas of the 5th Methodist Mission and Domingo Martinez, living on the east side of Broad Street across from Spring Garden, their neighborhoods in Northern Liberties also began to reflect a progressive influx of Puerto Ricans. In formation since the interwar years, this core group of leaders from the business, community and religious sectors, worked to help the newer arrivals from Puerto Rico during the 1950s. The next twenty-five years were crucial in the development of a more distinctively Puerto Rican community.

This chapter explores the legacies that the interwar era provided for the Great Migration of the post-World War II era. As has been documented by several scholars, the large wave of Puerto Ricans who came to the City of Philadelphia after WW II was due, in part, to labor migration policies undertaken by policymakers in Puerto Rico and the United States at the end of the war.[1] While Puerto Rico's policymakers sought to reduce what they defined as "overpopulation," U.S. policymakers sought to help U.S. employers meet what they defined as a "need" for cheap, seasonal labor. These government policies and labor recruitment programs, as well as the social networks that accompanied them, all echoed dimensions that had characterized the interwar period.

At the same time that the interwar community provided a foundation, the impact of such a massive influx from Puerto Rico on the migrants and their neighbors was significant. The previously diverse Latino enclaves were transformed as a more distinctly Puerto Rican community evolved in Philadelphia. Puerto Rican neighborhoods shifted, with some growing rapidly and some shrinking. The city took notice of its Puerto Rican residents. During the war, an increase in the level of economic activity coupled with a major increase in Puerto Rican migration enhanced the organizational developments of the period. Community development continued to evolve in the postwar period, sometimes building on interwar antecedents and sometimes taking new directions. The migration of diverse Latino groups increased beginning in the late 1960s, making Philadelphia more Pan-Latino, that is, more like it was in the early twentieth century when Puerto Ricans first arrived. The Puerto Rican community was now in the role of assisting other Latino groups in the city. This epilogue begins to chart these legacies and the shifts that came to characterize Puerto Rican Philadelphia from the Great Migration to the present.

The Great Migration to Philadelphia

Important political and economic developments on the island in the immediate years after the end of the war and labor needs in the U.S. helped to shape migration to the U.S. This was particularly true in the Pennsylvania and Southern New Jersey regions. Building on precedents like the recruitment of Puerto Rican workers to the Campbell Soup Company, Puerto Rico's Migration Division collaborated with the U.S. Employment Service to facilitate the migration of first hundreds and then thousands of Puerto Ricans to the area for seasonal farm work (Whalen 2001: 76, 78–9). Coupled with the informal familial networks, as has been discussed in previous chapters, some formed before WW II, the number of Puerto Ricans in Philadelphia increased dramatically by the early 1950s, as more Puerto Ricans came directly to Philadelphia once airline flights from Puerto Rico became available. As a result, Puerto Ricans came to Philadelphia directly from Puerto Rico, from the farms of Pennsylvania and southern New Jersey, and at times, from New York City or other parts of the United States. Between 1940 and 1954, the Puerto Rican population in the city increased from approximately 1,000 to more than 7,300. The Puerto Rican community of Philadelphia blossomed into the third largest concentration in the United States behind those of New York City and Chicago (O'Brien 1957).

Another important factor that explains an increasing dispersal of Puerto Rican migrants throughout the U.S. in this postwar period has to do with the policies instituted by Puerto Rico's policymakers, who decided to help distribute migrants away from places like New York City. In the late 1940s and early 1950s, the vast majority of Puerto Ricans heading to the U.S. went to New York City. Officials there took notice and raised concerns about the challenges of integrating this new, multiracial, Spanish-speaking population, who were also U.S. citizens. The Migration Division of Puerto Rico placed an emphasis on sending contract laborers to other locations away from New York, including Connecticut, Illinois, Ohio, Pennsylvania, Southern New Jersey, among others.[2] As Puerto Rican scholar Jose Hernandez Alvarez argues, the ploy worked: while many Puerto Ricans continued to travel to New York, many also moved to other parts of the U.S. (Hernández Álvarez 1968).

In the postwar era, many Puerto Ricans found a segmented labor market in Philadelphia divided by gender and race.[3] Women like Carmen Aponte and Tomasita Romero, among others, went to work in the clothing industry. Earlier Puerto Rican migrants had experienced a segmented labor market in the inter-war period, as well as the beginnings of deindustrialization. These earlier occupational patterns and economic shifts were an indicator of things to come. As deindustrialization continued, Puerto Ricans' plight in post-industrial Philadelphia became particularly evident in North Philadelphia, where Aponte and Romero found garment factories upon their arrival. By the 1980s, most were gone. This economic segmentation and the economic shifts, rooted in the interwar era, are important for understanding the Puerto Rican community's development and the jobs they were relegated to within the broader confines of a racially divided city (Whalen 2001: 143; Perillan 1990: 4–5; Serrano 1994).

Settlements and an increasing awareness of Puerto Ricans

With the Great Migration, Puerto Rican settlement in the city shifted, as some neighborhoods saw fewer Puerto Ricans settling and others saw dramatic increases. The significant increase of Puerto Ricans in Philadelphia during the early 1950s had been noted by some community agencies and a few city officials as well. But the primary proponents and advocacy efforts on behalf of the community were led by Dr. DeCelis, longtime resident of the city, and businessman Domingo Martinez. Up until the early 1950s, most Philadelphians, including many local officials, took little notice of the Puerto Rican influx. This would change in the summer of 1953. Two events led to bringing the Puerto Rican community of Philadelphia to the attention of the rest of the City. In particular, an incident in Spring Garden ushered in an era of studies of the Puerto Rican community and social service responses, by city officials and Puerto Rican community leaders (Siegel, Orlan and Greer 1975).

Along with spectacular growth came a geographic shift in Puerto Rican residency. Shifting away from the Spring Garden area, Puerto Rican settlements grew in the area east of Broad Street and north along 5th Street and into the heart of North Philadelphia. This new area contained some of the most dilapidated housing in North Philadelphia. By 1960, there were 14,424 Puerto Ricans living in Philadelphia according to the U.S. Census. This number represented a doubling of the population since 1954. It was, by any account a very dramatic increase and these trends continued, as the Puerto Rican community became more geographically compact and socially complex between the late 1960s and 1980s (City of Philadelphia 1964: 6). Caught up in the racial binary of Philadelphia at the time, which was approximately 40 percent African American community and the white ethnic community, which also made up another 40 percent of the population, Puerto Ricans became more isolated (Gonzalez 1987–88: 37).[4]

During this period, a process of gentrification began to take place in several areas of the city close to Center City. Spring Garden, among others, was greatly affected by this making it a contributing factor to the exodus of Puerto Ricans from this community. By the end of the 1980s, there were only a few blocks left in Spring Garden where Puerto Ricans resided. But during the 1950s this was an area undergoing dramatic change in contested ways. It was here that the city took notice of the increasing numbers of Puerto Ricans in the city.

Philadelphia takes note of Puerto Rican presence in the City
On the night of July 17, 1953, a fight between Puerto Rican and white ethnic residents of the Spring Garden neighborhood led to rioting and street fighting that lasted more than a week. Although it was fairly evident that racist attitudes of white neighbors led to the conflict, the City's newly created Philadelphia Commission on Human Relations (PCHR) treated the matter as a conflict sparked by a lack of understanding between old established (white) residents and the newly arrived Puerto Rican (foreign) neighbors. The incident hastened the first study of the Puerto Rican community by PCHR, which had initially been requested by the Puerto Rican leadership, and led to the creation of the Committee on Puerto Rican Affairs (CPRA) of the Health and Welfare Council. The CPRA was made up primarily of leaders of the Puerto Rican community and city officials (Siegel, Orlan and Greer 1975; *Philadelphia Evening Bulletin* 1954: 3; *Philadelphia Inquirer* 1954: 5).[5]

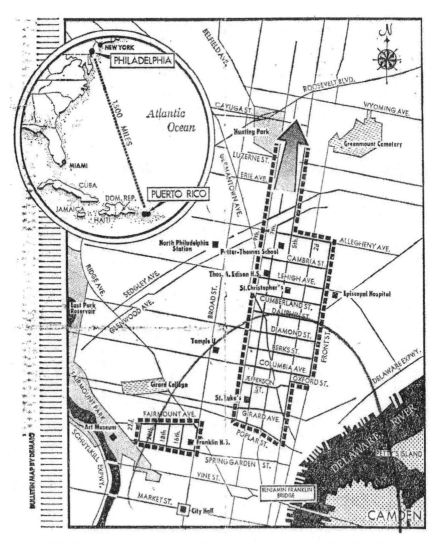

Map 3. This reflects the growth the Puerto Rican community in North Philadelphia, there is no reference to the Puerto Rican settlement in Southward, ca.1970.

A week later, on July 25, 1953, the Puerto Rican community marked the first an-niversary of the establishment of the Commonwealth status of Puerto Rico. Celebrated during the backdrop of the street fighting of the previous week, the event stood in stark contrast to the riot. A speech by then Island Governor, Luis Munoz Marin, was broadcast on a loudspeaker directly across from City Hall where the celebration took place. Dr. Jose DeCelis was the chairman of the organizing committee, and the newly formed American Legion Latin American Post #840 was the color guard for the event. These two events marked an important step in the evolution of the Puerto Rican community in Philadelphia because of the attention they brought to themselves through local media and political officials. This was the first time the city had paid this much attention to or even recognized the Puerto Ricans in their midst. This previous invisibility of the local Puerto Rican community was about to change (Whalen 2001: 204–5).

The first formal study of the Puerto Rican community in Philadelphia was conducted by the Philadelphia Commission on Human Relations (PCHR), in the aftermath of the Spring Garden street fighting incident during the previous summer. Although the PCHR had announced that it would undertake such a study before the fighting occurred, it was clear that the effort by the Commission became more urgent as a result of the clashes. The study became the first effort of Philadelphia to come to terms with defining whether or not it had a "Puerto Rican Problem." While City officials did not recognize a "problem" per se, the results of the Commission's study failed to recognize the blatant racism that existed in the City at the time and concluded that the street fighting between Puerto Ricans and their white neighbors in Spring Garden was the result of Puerto Rican's "problem of adjustments." As a result, policymakers decided to "help" Puerto Ricans adjust to their new environment so they could better fit in with their neighbors. While the report did recognize that a "moderate amount of prejudice" existed against Puerto Ricans by their white neighbors, the emphasis of the Commission's conclusions and remedy was to help Puerto Ricans "adjust." Nothing in the report, however, suggests that any emphasis to directly confront the racial attitudes of the white residents of Spring Garden needed to be addressed (Whalen 2001: 194; Siegel, Orlan and Greer 1975: 61).

Puerto Rican leaders of the interwar era, including Dr. DeCelis and businessman Domingo Martinez, continued to play important roles in the community. These leaders had held meetings in March and then again in May 1953 at the International Institute to discuss how local organizations could assist the growing Puerto Rican population and help meet its needs. All of those present at these meetings agreed that a serious and deliberate study about the community and its needs was required in order to better determine how to assist. It was at that time that the PCHR agreed to take on the responsibility of conducting said study, and Puerto Rican community leaders, along with representatives from the local office of the Migration Division of Puerto Rico and La Milagrosa, as well as representatives from city agencies, participated in the design of the study (Siegel, Orlan and Greer 1975: 7–8).

As a consequence of the PCHR study, the local Health and Welfare Council organized the Committee on Puerto Rican Affairs (CPRA). The CPRA was formally established in October 1954 and was made up of members of the Puerto Rican community and representatives of social and civic groups interested in the welfare of the Puerto Rican community. The first chairman of the CPRA was Dr. Jose DeCelis. He served in this capacity until 1957. Other members of the CPRA included Domingo Martinez; the Reverend Enrique Rodriguez, Spanish Baptist Church; Carmen Aponte, 5th Street Community Center; and Carlos Martinez, Camden Field Office, Puerto Rico Migration Division. They served alongside Anna McGarry, Philadelphia Commission on Human Relations; Dr. Alfred S. Boguch, District Health Services; Eleanor Lafton, Department of Public Nursing; Mr. and Mrs. Eugenio Mutt; and Charles Sierra (Metauten 1959: 26; Wells 1958: 2).[6] The charge of the Committee was to generate interest in "dealing with problems concerning individual Puerto Ricans and/or the Puerto Rican community as a whole." In addition, it was the purpose of the Committee to "facilitate the assimilation of Philadelphia's Puerto Rican population in the community." Serving as a clearing house for the community, CPRA published bilingual materials on important city services; organized meetings with city officials; worked with the Philadelphia Commission on Human Relations and helped to send city officials from key agencies to Puerto Rico to learn more about Puerto Rican culture (Metauten 1959: 26).

By the mid-1950s, the leadership of the Puerto Rican community was advocating to the Mayor's Office for the hiring of bilingual staff to ease communications with the community, and in a meeting with community leaders, Mayor Richardson Dilworth committed to do this. In addition, the mayor asked his friend, academic Dr. Henry Wells of the University of Pennsylvania, to prepare a report on the Puerto Rican community and make recommendations. At the time (1957), Wells was a professor of political science, but the mayor also tapped him because of Wells' firsthand knowledge of Puerto Rico and Puerto Ricans. Wells had lived in Puerto Rico for a few years and had been a close ally of the last American Governor of Puerto Rico, Rexford G. Tugwell, during his tenure on the island (1941–1946). Wells had also taught at the University of Puerto Rico and had written a book about the island, So Mayor Dilworth was confident Wells could produce the report he needed (Wells 1958, 2000).

Dr. Wells completed his study in February 1958. For the study, Wells interviewed more than forty city and state officials, as well as the leadership of the Committee on Puerto Rican Affairs. He concluded, among other things, that Puerto Ricans in Philadelphia resembled other previous immigrant groups in that "their economic, social, and cultural factors peculiar to themselves made it difficult in making a rapid and successful adjustment to life in the city.". Puerto Rican's social adjustment, argued Wells, had been "impeded by shortcomings in "the lack of adults learning English," as well as difficulties in "employment services…and housing." The quotations suggest that Puerto Ricans had serious deficiencies common to other immigrant groups and that it was a matter of improving communications (presumably Puerto Ricans vis-a-vis the rest of the city). In order for the lives of Puerto Ricans to improve, Dr. Wells recommended to the mayor three things: (1) intensify and improve existing services to Puerto Ricans by increasing the number of English language acquisition classes for adults taught by bilingual personnel; have city agencies recruit bilingual personnel; and send city personnel to Puerto Rico during summer for workshops to learn more about the culture; (2) hire one or two liaison officers for the city, bilingual in English and Puerto Rican-Spanish (sic), to serve as a link to the community and public and private agencies of the city; and (3) establish a Newcomer's Bureau for Puerto Ricans. Later in the study, Wells described these actions further. It is not clear if the mayor adopted all of Wells's recommendations, but a city liaison was eventually hired (Wells 1958: ii–iii).

Also, as a result of the PCHR 1954 study, the Catholic Archdiocese of Philadelphia announced the opening of a settlement house called Case del Carmen to serve Puerto Ricans in the city. In a *Philadelphia Evening Bulletin* article, Archbishop John F. O'Hare confirmed the purchase of a three-story house located at 7th and Jefferson streets and appointed the Rev. Fredric H. Hickey as director. Father Hickey had once lived in Puerto Rico and for the previous ten years had taught at the Roman Catholic high school in Philadelphia (*Philadelphia Evening Bulletin* 1954). Thus, the on-going efforts of Puerto Rican leaders from the interwar era coincided with the events in the summer of 1953 to increase the city's awareness of Puerto Ricans in the city. Working with city officials, these Puerto Rican leaders, joined by newly arriving Puerto Ricans, encouraged an increase in services to the city's rapidly expanding Puerto Rican population. Clearly the efforts of a Puerto Rican leadership and its advocacy on behalf of their community began to bear fruit.

Community Roots and New Directions

As the Puerto Rican community grew during the 1950s and 1960s, so did its organizational efforts. Supported by leaders from La Milagrosa, the First Spanish Baptist Church, and La Fraternal, new groups began to evolve, especially town-based social clubs representing the migrants' hometown back on the island. Protestant churches also were established. In the late 1940s, both Jose DeCelis and Domingo Martinez emerged as leaders that arriving Puerto Ricans sought out for help. Along with Mary Rodriguez, who had become a lay nun at La Milagrosa; the Reverend Enrique Rodriguez at the Spanish Baptist Church, as well as Samuel Freedman's work with farmworkers and laborers; and Antonio Malpica's cultural hub in the Tenderloin section and Domingo Martinez' grocery store in Northern Liberties, Puerto Ricans found an array of support networks in this postwar period. Over the decades, new avenues for community building were taken, including increasingly political ones as Puerto Ricans began to participate in the electoral arena.

Throughout the 1950s, leaders of the Committee on Puerto Rican Affairs like Carmen Aponte, who had come to Philadelphia in 1947, Domingo Martinez, and the Reverend Enrique Rodriguez, among others, struggled to get the city to address the many needs of the Puerto Rican community. The limited progress on these fronts eventually led to the formation of the Council of Spanish Speaking Organizations, El Concilio, in 1962. The Concilio, currently the oldest Puerto Rican/Latino social service agency in Philadelphia, initially brought together many diverse Latino community groups under one Pan-Latino organization made up mostly of Puerto Ricans, but inclusive of all Latinos in La Fraternal. In 1968, the Concilio became the first full social service agency funded by city and federal funds. Outreach to the Puerto Rican community through city agencies and religious organizations improved. So did the cultural and political life of the Puerto Rican community. Puerto Ricans made small inroads into the political arena when some of them were elected as the first committeemen and women (Whalen 2001: 216–7).

Founded on October 1, 1962 (and incorporated in 1967), the Concilio became a federation of different Latino groups in the City. This was the first time such an effort of this type had taken place. Originally, about half a dozen groups formed the Concilio but, by 1968 there were thirteen affiliates, and by 1976 there were 21 member organizations. The Concilio's mission established four main areas of concern: (1) addressing issues of police/community relations; (2) employment; (3) housing; and (4) social services. It began as an advocacy group in these areas and led the effort to establish bilingual programs in Philadelphia public schools and develop bilingual information handouts about city government offices among others (Farr 1994).

The 1960s were also marked by an expansion of the civil rights movement that led to the Civil Rights Act (1964) and the Voting Rights Act (1965). This period was ushered in by President Lyndon Johnson's Great Society initiative, intended to increase the role of the federal government in programs like the War on Poverty. Beginning in 1967, the Concilio became a social service provider through federal grants. In 1968, the Concilio inaugurated a multi-service program, Project Welcome. This

project allowed the Concilio to hire full-time staff, including job developers and social workers. This was Concilio's first federally funded program, and the funds were
provided by the Office of Economic Opportunity and awarded by the Philadelphia
Anti-Poverty Action Commission (PAAC) (Farr 1994: 4). Also, in 1964, the Concilio
began a tradition that has remained a highlight of the Puerto Rican community and
cultural pride: The Annual Puerto Rican Day Parade. In the 1960s, several Puerto Ricans ran for political office. In 1968, German Quiles was elected to the Pennsylvania
General Assembly, and others like Hilda Arteaga and Jose Hernandez were elected
committeemen and -women. The Concilio also founded an Aspira chapter in 1969, a
Puerto Rican leadership and educational organization originally from New York, as
well as the 5th Street Merchants Association.

By the end of the 1980s, the predominant social and political life of Puerto
Ricans was wielded by the Concilio. The Concilio, argued Juan Gonzalez in his
article, was very tight with the Mayor of Philadelphia, Frank Rizzo. Rizzo, a former
police commissioner ran the city as a virtual police state (Gonzalez 1987–88: 37).
Several high profile cases of racial discrimination against Puerto Ricans occurred
during these years, and a group of young Puerto Rican activists began to mobilize
the community seeking social justice. Some of the more salient cases included that
of Julio Osorio, a handicapped junior high school student, who in 1973 was thrown
in the Delaware River by a gang of white youths and drowned (*Philadelphia Evening
Bulletin* 1973).[7] That same year a group of Puerto Ricans was arrested and tried in a
sensational rape and murder case of a young white girl and her boyfriend near the
Art Museum in Spring Garden. All were convicted and sentenced to many years in
jail. Then, in the late 1970s, six people died when the home of the Santiago family,
who lived in the Feltonville section of the city, a white neighborhood, had their
home firebombed (McCaffrey and Ridgeway 1975; Camp and Gillespie 1975; Gillespie 1975; Lewis 1975; Gunter 1975). And there was also the case of José Reyes
who was shot by the police in 1977. "Throughout these events," argues Gonzalez,
"the Concilio leadership failed to defend our rights."[8]

Beginning in the 1970s, during the height of the black liberation and anti-Viet-
nam War movements, elements in the Philadelphia Puerto Rican community began
to organize direct-action groups. Made up of the sons and daughters of the pioneer
Puerto Rican migrants of the 1930s, 1940s, and 1950s, this second generation of
"Philly-Ricans" began to protest conditions in the community and, in some cases, to
confront the established community leadership—accusing them of being too conser-
vative and conformist. In the early 1970s and 80s, two such groups came into prominence: the Philadelphia chapter of the Young Lords Party (YLP); and the Puerto Ri-

can Socialist Party. Both organizations led protest marches to demand city services for the Puerto Rican community (Whalen 2001; 221; Gonzalez 1987–88).[9]

A group of aspirantes, who were also artists, founded Taller Puertorriqueño in 1974. The Taller would eventually emerge as a major cultural center in the Barrio. Also, in 1971 a group of students at Temple University, calling themselves the Puerto Rican Student Federation, began a campaign for the increased recruitment of minority students. The Federation, led by Rudy Arson, Jose Navarro, Julio Olmo and Idalie Munoz, among others, protested in the president's office. Another student who lent support to the undergrads was a Puerto Rican Law student from New York, Nelson Diaz, who later became an attorney and judge. The students won some concessions: increased recruitment of Puerto Rican students and staff and a Puerto Rican Studies Program. Olmo would go on to run for Elections Commissioner citywide and came very close to being elected on the Republican Party ticket (Olmo 2013; *Philadelphia Evening Bulletin* 1971).

The Philadelphia Chapter of the Puerto Rican Socialist Party (PSP) stood for independence and socialism on the island; it viewed the Puerto Rican diaspora as part of the Puerto Rican Nation. In the U.S., the PSP organized chapters in several cities where there were large concentrations of Puerto Ricans. In addition, to organizing support for the struggles of the island, *pesepeistas* (members of the PSP) in the U.S. organized around the struggles of their respective community's democratic rights. The Philadelphia chapter, led by Ben Ramos, Rafaela Colon, Mario Rivera and Wilfredo Rojas, among others, focused their work on protesting police brutality, promoting bilingual education and better housing, etc. Ramos eventually would be selected as a Deputy Mayor in the City and later became a member of the Pennsylvania General Assembly (Ramos 2013).

A major turning point during this period of social and political activism came in 1978. During that year, Mayor Rizzo, in his second term, due to expire in 1980, decided to challenge the two-term limit and change the city charter so he could run again. His decision emboldened a broad opposition led by liberal whites, the African American community and Puerto Rican activists. A coalition of Puerto Rican activists who had grown up in Philadelphia and a few transplanted Nuyorican activists as well as some new arrivals from the island formed the backbone of Rizzo's opposition in the barrio. These activists coalesced in a group called Puerto Ricans United against Rizzo (PRUAR). They launched a massive voter registration drive in the community. At the time there were approximately five thousand Puerto Ricans registered to vote. After the drive, there were more than ten thousand. On Election Day, more than 60 percent of Puerto Ricans voted against Rizzo, and the charter amendment was defeated (Gonzalez 1987–88: 38).

After the election of 1979, the PRUAR coalition held a Puerto Rican convention and established the Puerto Rican Alliance (PRA). The PRA became a mass civil rights organization and for the next few years led massive squatter's campaigns, organized and supported labor strikes involving Puerto Rican workers and campaigned against the U.S. Navy bombardment of the island-town of Vieques in Puerto Rico. The Alliance also got involved in local politics running candidates for the State legislature and City Council. In 1984, these efforts bore fruit as Ralph Acosta, a PRA founder, won a seat on the Pennsylvania General Assembly, and in 1985, attorney and also PRA founder Angel L. Ortiz was elected to the Philadelphia City Council. By 1990, more than thirty thousand Puerto Ricans were registered to vote in Philadelphia (Gonzalez 1987–88: 47; Whalen 1998: 122).

The campaigns of the Puerto Rican Alliance contributed to opening opportunities for Puerto Ricans in the decade of the 1980s. In 1981, attorney and Temple Law School graduate Nelson A. Diaz was appointed judge of the Court of Common Pleas. In 1985, Mayor W. Wilson Goode, the first African American mayor of the city of Philadelphia, appointed Dr. Christine Torres Matrullo as the first Puerto Rican to serve on the Philadelphia School Board. However, despite these important political gains, a Temple University study on the Puerto Rican community in Philadelphia published in 1985 found that the community lagged behind blacks and whites in terms of economic status, educational attainment, labor force participation and housing segregation in the city (Gonzalez 1987–88: 41; Ericksen et al 1985: iv–vi). During this period, a group of former employees of the Concilio broke with the organization and founded the Asociación de Puertorriqueños en Marcha (APM) and the Congreso de Latinos Unidos. Both of these groups would become major social services agencies and compete for funds with the Concilio. In addition to these new social services agencies, the work of the Puerto Rican Alliance in Philadelphia stimulated the formation of a national civil rights groups called the National Congress for Puerto Rican Rights (NCPRR), founded in 1981. Its first President was Juan Gonzalez, the former founder of the Young Lords in New York and founding member of the Puerto Rican Alliance in Philadelphia. The NCPRR would go on to exist for 30 years and lead national and local campaigns for bilingual education, fair redistricting processes, among others.

Pan-Latino Community Re-emerges

Just as in the early 1900s, in the early twenty-first century, Philadelphia's community became increasingly Pan-Latino with the arrival of increasing numbers of Dominicans, Colombians, Venezuelans, Peruvians, and Mexicans, among others. Organizations such as the Concilio and the Congreso de Latinos Unidos reached out to

Mexican residents in South Philadelphia and to Colombians and Dominicans in the northern sections of the city, providing them with needed social services. In this regard, although Puerto Ricans continue to predominate as a group, the Pan-Latino nature of the community has once again provided the backdrop for working across national lines in the interest of all Latinos in the city of Philadelphia.

During the 1990s, the Latino community continued to grow, yet the Puerto Rican population, still dominant in terms of numbers, began to cope with an increase in diversity among other Spanish speakers. Members of these respective groups reflected this growth in the establishment of a variety of organizations. The Dominican Community Cultural Center, founded to provide social services, was initially set up in the basement of the Incarnation Catholic Church in Olney and later moved to more permanent quarters at El Concilio in Northern Liberties. Meanwhile, the Colombian community experienced unprecedented growth as many left the war-torn country. Along with pioneers who had lived in Philadelphia for decades, Colombian immigrants formed business and social organizations such as the Colombian Coalition and began two weekly Spanish-language newspapers, *Al Dia*, founded by Hernan Guaracao and *El Sol Latino*, founded by Ricardo Hurtado, among others. During this period there was also a marked increase in the number of Central Americans, especially Guatemalans. Places like La Iglesia de Cristo y San Ambrosio, a Spanish-speaking Episcopal church in Hunting Park, opened its doors to this group with the Proyecto Sin Fronteras, an adult basic education program.

Despite the gains made by the Puerto Rican community, it lagged behind other groups in terms of most social and economic indicators. During the summer of 1990, for instance, the Philadelphia Human Relations Commission conducted public hearings regarding the concerns of the Philadelphia Latino community. Prompted by incidents of racial violence from the previous summer, dozens of Puerto Rican residents testified to the lack of adequate city attention given to Puerto Ricans in the areas of health and human services, the judicial system, employment and economic development, fire and police departments and recreation, among others. According to the testimony provided by Councilman Angel L. Ortiz, who was the first speaker at the hearings, "Puerto Ricans still do not play a role in the City government... there is a strong feeling in the community that City government has consciously maintained institutional barriers to prevent Latinos from securing employment and obtaining city services." For his part, Judge Nelson Diaz added, "We are continually abused and used by the political process" (Philadelphia Human Relations Commission 1991: 3; II-1, III-1).

The PCHR study of 1990 was again sparked by separate incidents of racial/ethnic conflicts which rocked the city in the summer of 1989. In May, a young white male named Sean Daily was killed in a case of mistaken identity when a group made up mostly of Puerto Rican youths descended upon a group of white youth one night in the Port Richmond sector of the city. The attack had been provoked by a previous incident of violence from a group of white youths against a member of the Puerto Rican group. Unfortunately for Daily, who was not part of the original incident, he lost his life in the attack. Eleven of the attackers, ten Puerto Ricans and a mixed race (black/white) youth were summarily arrested and charged with first-degree murder. Two months later, in the Feltonville section of the city, near where the Santiago family's house had been burned a decade earlier, another violent encounter between Puerto Ricans and whites took the life of Stephen Crespo. In this particular case, only one of the white perpetrators was arrested and charged with 3rd degree manslaughter.

Loud protests organized by a group called the Puerto Rican Justice Defense Coalition led by Patricia DeCarlo and Victor Vazquez rallied support and eventually got the PCHR involved. In yet another study by the Commission, the results indicated that Puerto Ricans/Latinos were in fact still underrepresented in city government, most city agencies, as well as colleges and universities in the city. Notwithstanding, the community has made some headway on this front. Nelson Diaz became City Solicitor of Philadelphia followed by Ken Trujillo; Alba Martinez, an attorney, headed the Department of Human Services and Pedro Ramos became the first Puerto Rican to chair the Philadelphia School Board.

Certain sectors of the Puerto Rican community, especially in North Philadelphia, began to show signs of an increasingly diverse Latino population. Gone were the days of a dominant presence of Puerto Rican grocery store owners. Dominicans purchased those grocery stores, many financed by their Asociación de Bodegueros Dominicanos, a mutual aid and business association made up of Dominican grocery store owners. This organization played an active role in the Latino community in support of mayoral democratic candidate Michael Nutter (Ortiz 2007). Nutter won the Democratic Party primary and the general election in 2007. In that same election Puerto Ricans elected the first Latina to City Council, Maria Quinones-Sanchez, a native Puerto Rican of Philadelphia's Hunting Park section.

Mexican farm laborers, who began to replace Puerto Rican laborers in the outlying areas of Philadelphia, surpassed them in the 1990s. By the year 2000, Mexican farm workers, especially from the State of Michoacán, constituted the absolute majority of laborers in Philadelphia's outlying areas and in southern New Jersey. Subsequently, as Puerto Ricans did before them, these Mexican laborers discovered better-paying jobs in the restaurants and hotels of the burgeoning Philadelphia hospitality and tourism industry. This fact lured them to the city. There, the local community has organized Casa Guadalupe, a multi-service, nonprofit entity. Also, through the help of the local consulate, a Mexican cultural center has been formed.

Conclusion

This chapter helps to bridge the gap in the literature between the interwar and postwar communities, a shortcoming in existing scholarship that focuses on postwar migration only. This study confirms just how significant the role was played by that early organizational migration experience in establishing an important beachhead on which the post-World War II migration landed. These early pioneers set the tone for negotiating this community space with the larger, often hostile, non-Hispanic community of cities like Philadelphia. The bulk of available literature on Puerto Ricans in the U.S. misses this point entirely. This study, then, helps to fill the gap in that historiography and to connect the postwar migration (after 1945) and settlement expansion in Philadelphia to the earlier, up to now, relatively unknown migration. Second, this chapter adds additional information about the insertion and development of the postwar Puerto Rican community with data previously not used by scholars who have written about the Puerto Rican Great Migration to Philadelphia. It is the hope of this book to have introduced the readers to a broader spectrum of the Puerto Rican experiences in Philadelphia as well as to insert this community more broadly and firmly in the historical mosaic that is the City of Philadelphia in the twenty-first century.

NOTES

Chapter 1

[1] A good example of theory literature on Puerto Ricans in Philadelphia is Siegel, Orlan and Greer 1975).

[2] I use the term "Pan-Hispanic" as a way to denote that in the late nineteenth and early twentieth century Philadelphia while there were several Spanish –speaking groups in the city including Puerto Ricans the largest group was from Spain. Progressively more Puerto Ricans began arriving in larger numbers and by the 1940s became the premier Spanish-speaking group in the City.

[3] For the purpose of this book, "enclave" is used to distinguish small groups of Spanish-speaking settlers who lived in geographic areas of approximately five city blocks by ten city blocks. The density of the enclave varied but it could stretch from several families and respective boarders to several hundred people.

[4] Mary and Tomas Rodriguez were married on 29 June 1931, in Manhattan, New York, Marriage Certificate #161565, New York Marriage Index 1866-1937. Accessed through www. Ancestry.com 6 June 2016.

[5] Examples of the use of the increasingly extensive archival material in the Centro Archives include Jesús Colón *The Way It Was and Other Writings* (1993), co-edited by Edna Acosta-Belén and Virginia Sánchez Korrol. This book was published posthumously and represents only a handful of the more than 250 essays or sketches included in the Jesús Colón (1901–1974) Papers donated to the Center for Puerto Rican Studies. Colón, a contemporary and friend of Bernardo Vega was a prolific writer and journalist and important figure in the early history of Puerto Ricans. He published an earlier collection of his "sketches" depicting Puerto Rican life in this period. His *Puerto Ricans in New York and Other Sketches* (1961) was not well known nor widely distributed, probably because Colón was an active member of the Communist Party of the U.S. Other writings of the 1990s also reflect a growing interest in the earlier period of Puerto Rican migration. These writings include essays like Ortiz (1996) and Delgado (1998).

[6] In addition to works already cited see: Ortiz (1996); Centro de Estudios Puertorriqueños (1982); Rodríguez-Morazzani (1994–95) and Glasser (1994–95). For comparative possibilities aside from the already cited works by Sánchez Korrol (1994) and Glasser 1994–95, 1995, 1997, see Carr (1989).

[7] The Merriam-Webster dictionary defines enclave as a: "territorial or culturally distinct unit enclosed within a foreign territory." In the case of this study, these culturally distinct (Spanish-speaking) units sometimes comprised an area only a few square blocks and where several dozen families resided.

Chapter 2

[1] Trade volume between Puerto Rico and the United States increased from a total $269,008 in 1813 to $1,082,299 in 1816 and to $2,103,498 by 1818 (Morales Carrión 1984: 69).

[2] For a detail description of this episode see Doucoudray Holstein (1829).

[3] For a look at the text of the first seven issues of *El Habanero* see Varela y Morales (1997).

4 This organization was founded by Cuban and Puerto Rican exiles in New York on 21 December 1865.

5 For an excellent chronology of the development of the Partido Revolucionario Cubano (PRC) activities between 1892 and 1898 in Philadelphia, see the microfilm collection of *Patria*, the Party paper, located at the Center for Puerto Rican Studies, Hunter College, CUNY. For a description of the role-played by Puerto Ricans within the PRC see Melendez (1995). For fine accounts U.S. intervention in Cuba, especially the role it played in the war between the Cuban insurgents and the Spanish colonial authorities see the books by Cuban historian Pérez (1990, 1993).

6 In a list of members of the Partido Revolucionario Cubano published in *Patria,* January 18, 1898, microfilm collection, Centro de Estudios Puertorriqueños Archives, Hunter College, CUNY.

7 There are a fair amount of books and articles, which document cigar makers' organizational abilities and the many mutual aid societies they built in the United States. For detail efforts see: Vega (1984: chapters 6, 7 and 8); Mormino and Pozzetta (1987: chapter 6; 1993: 10); Schneider (1994: chapter 3); Greenbaum (1993: 173); Martínez (1989: 75).

8 The *Cigar Makers Official Journal* (*CMOJ*) "reported a union of Spanish and Cuban cigar makers in Philadelphia in 1877 (see *CMOJ*, Dec., 1877, p. 1—cited in Cooper 1987).

9 Puerto Rican Sotero Figueroa edited *Patria*, the Cuban Revolutionary Party newspaper, published in New York from 1892 until 1898. The leadership listings for Philadelphia based groups are taken from three editions dates: (illegible), 1892; July 22, 1893 and October 5, 1895. For listings of occupations of the leadership see Philadelphia City Directories: 1892, 1893 and 1895.

10 Many of the members of the PRC in Philadelphia formed organizations like the Hispanic-American Fraternal Association.

11 For example, between 1898 and 1910 alone there were 33 major labor strikes on the island. Artisan groups of which cigar makers led 10 led most of these strikes (Tirado n.d.: 3–4—cited with author's permission). For a brief description of the changes that the cigar making industries underwent in this period see Montgomery (1987: 151, 196).

12 In addition, see Puerto Rican newspaper accounts at the time, especially *La Correspondencia* (1919, 11 January: 1).

13 Alfaro (1983: 10) argues that the Puerto Rican presence in southern New Jersey in the 1920s was due to agricultural contracts that brought them from the island to this region after World War I. Also, see Colón-Colón (1983: 7). Both works cited in Aponte et al. (1994: 35–6).

14 There would, however be no more construction boom again in Philadelphia until the 1950s.

15 War Manpower Commission, National Archives, Philadelphia Region, Record Group 211, Box 2299, File 1. (Hereafter cited as WMC)

16 For description of the role played by the Campbell Soup Company in the war effort see several numbers of *Soup Tureen*, the company's newsletter. In particular, see the letter written by Arthur C. Dorrance, General Manager of Campbell entitled, "Our Plans for 1943", in which he outlines labor shortages and needs while putting in a pitch for help, especially from housewives in the neighborhood. The crunch period was expected in the summer when the tomato crops came in and not enough workers were available for unloading the trucks. Other numbers of this newsletter describe labor shortage and, the enormous need to handle produce that would arrive that summer, particularly tomatoes and some numbers offered prizes and bonuses to employees

for helping to recruit seasonal workers, see especially *Soup Tureen* for June, July, August, September and October, 1943. Campbell Soup Archives, Camden, New Jersey, hereafter cited as CSA. (I am indebted to Campbell Archivist Jan Sickler for providing copies of the newsletters.)
[17] For a detail description of the process of bringing in workers for Campbell Soup and other area businesses during the year consult WMC records located in the National Archives Regional Center in Philadelphia.
[18] See also WMC Record Group 211, Box 2333, file 6-2-3, which contains lists of several hundred Puerto Rican employees who left their jobs, breaking their respective contracts with the Campbell Soup Company, the Edgar Hurff Canning Company and the Baltimore & Ohio Railroad, especially in the latter's Pennsylvania area operations.
[19] WMC, folder 6-2-3, especially letters from Puerto Rican and WMC officials who visited numerous work sites and spoke to the laborers themselves. Some of the Puerto Rican officials even agreed that the workers had legitimate reasons for concern
[20] Joan D. Koss and Juan Giusti, among others, claim that it was these workers who actually founded the Puerto Rican community in Philadelphia. My argument, however, disproves that but the fact is that many of these workers did find their way to Philadelphia, where they had friends and/or family in the "colonia". Many became members of Reverend Enrique Rodriguez' First Spanish Baptist Mission in Philadelphia.

Chapter 3

1 Dones was 29 years old at the time and was married to Bienvenida Barzilay.
2 Massey argues that an increase in a groups poverty rates, Blacks and Puerto Ricans in the case of his essay, inevitably produces a concentration of poverty when it occurs under conditions of high segregation. Following this argument, Whalen in her study on the Puerto Rican community in the post-World War II period argues that in U.S. urban centers Blacks and Puerto Ricans were the only groups who simultaneously experienced high levels of segregation *and* sharp increase in poverty. My argument in this chapter is to broadly outline how residential segregation of Blacks and Puerto Ricans in Philadelphia was evident in the changing residential patterns of the city during the period between 1910 and 1930 (Massey 1990: 331; Whalen 2001: 227).
3 In his study of the Black community in Cleveland, Kenneth L. Kusmer (1976: 41–5) found similar residential patterns evolve relative to segregation black and ethnic communities. Although some segregation of blacks in Cleveland existed before World War I, the pace quickened after migration of that period. Also, not all ethnic groups were dispersed throughout the city in this period. Yet, blacks became more segregated into communities clearly defined as "Negro sections" while, progressively, white ethnics were able to disperse throughout the city. The Philadelphia experience in this period also points to increased segregation for blacks, and though initially Latinos had similar experiences as other ethnic groups such as the Italians, the Polish and Russian Jews, as the city became more racially segregated, the residential experiences of Puerto Ricans and other Latinos took on the characteristics of black neighborhoods: older, deplorable housing, concentrated unskilled labor and poverty.
4 The concentration of Puerto Rican and other Spanish-speaker's residential patterns in the

period leading up to the Great Depression resembles the form of a letter "S". Beginning at the bottom (Grays Ferry and Southwark), the pattern snakes along northbound to also include parts of Society Hill, Chinatown, East Poplar, Northern Liberties, Spring Garden, Strawberry Mansion and West Kensington. In addition, there was another concentration in West Philadelphia, especially in Parkside with a smattering representation in the areas of Tioga and Hunting Park, north of Lehigh Avenue and in the east in Port Richmond.

5 Lacking consistent and systematic projections of the number of Spanish-speakers in Philadelphia during the first half of the twentieth century it was necessary to employ a method of population projection utilizing the available census data for 1910 through 1950, the manuscript census for 1910-1940, City Directories for the same period, Baptism and Marriage records from the Spanish-speaking Catholic Chapel Our Lady of the Miraculous Medal, "La Milagrosa" and the Chapel's year end reports, in which they estimated the number off Spanish-speaking Catholics in the city. On occasion, as in the case of the 1923 report, they estimated the number of Spanish-speakers in the city. In addition, having a working knowledge of the general migration and population trends for each of the Spanish-speaking groups to the United States helped in estimating population size for each one in the periods where no specific record existed. By and large, the biggest concentration of Spanish-speakers was located in the following wards: First through the Sixth, Twelfth through the Fifteenth, Twentieth, Twenty-eighth, Thirty-second, Thirty-eighth and Forty-seventh—see maps.

6 Department of Commerce,—Bureau of the Census—Fourteenth Census of the United States: 1920-Population. For Spanish-speakers in the area see especially Enumeration Districts 124 3B, 4B, 5A, and 8A.

7 "A Report on the Spanish Colony in Philadelphia," n.d., author unknown, found in NSC, Acc. #625, Box #63, Folder #11—Correspondence 1923–1925, p. 1 T.U.U.A. The report appears to have been written for the International Institute. It is possible that it was authored by the Fermina Martinez who in a letter to Olive Steede, Director of the International Institute, dated 23 February 1923, provided the information on the cigar making firms. A copy of said letter is included in the same folder as the "Report."; Boyd's Philadelphia City Directory, 1930. The two cigar making firms were located, one at 58 S. Second Street and the other at 623 S. Second Street.

8 Letter from Fermina Martinez to Olive Steede, International Institute dated 23 February 1923 describes different business endeavors of Spanish speakers in Philadelphia, NSC, Acc. #625, Box #63, Folder #11-Correspondence 1923–1925.

9 See in particular Enumeration Districts 210, 219 1B, 223 2A and 4A, 226 1B, 228 4A 229 9B for concentration of Spanish-speakers in the Fifteenth ward.

10 For other Puerto Ricans and Spanish-speakers in Spring Garden see especially Enumeration Districts 285–286 and 293–294.

11 The Spanish-surnames appear in Enumerator Districts #s 293 10 B, 11 B, and 13 A; 294 6 A and 7 A. In one residence 1636 Green Street, just a few short blocks from the Baldwin Locomotive Works' main building, Dr. Sebastian Romagosa, a dentist from Cuba who had immigrated in 1888 and became a naturalized citizen in 1895, ran his own business while his wife Jeannette ran a rooming house at the same address where fourteen Mexican, Cuban and Puerto

Rican males lived. All of these men worked for the Baldwin Locomotive Works.

[12] In a map produced in 1926 by the Mack Company of Philadelphia called "Ethnic Groups in Philadelphia", three areas were identified as being "Spanish": the two sectors in the tenderloin and a third enclave, in Southwark, with similar boundaries as the area also identified by Fermina Martinez in her letter to the International Institute in 1925. The map covers all of central Philadelphia, block by block. Each ethnic and racial group is identified by one color. There are more than three dozen such groups identified for the city. Temple University Urban Archives, Map Collection. For a vivid description of the tenderloin see Haller (1976: 283).

[13] On 23 May 1931 Antonio Malpica and his wife Mercedes Perez baptized their son Abelardo. Abelardo Malpica according to church records was born 8 October 1930 (Bermudez 1999).

[14] Domingo Martinez, according to Pedro Hernandez, a lifelong friend, arrived in Philadelphia in 1941. He went to work for a Spaniard who owned a grocery store in Northern Liberties and eventually opened up his own business in the Marshall Street area (Rodriguez 1999).

[15] See Population Enumeration District 293 11 in the First ward; Enumeration Districts 123, 124 5A, 124 2B, 124 3B, 124 4B, and 124 8A in the Fifth ward; Enumeration District 135 in the Sixth ward; Enumeration Districts 285 1B, 286 1B, 286 2B, 291 6B, 293 2B, 293 4B, 293 6B, 293 9B, 293 10B, 293 11B, 293 13A, 294 6A, 294 8A, 295 4B, 306 16B and 975 11A in the Fifteenth ward; Enumeration District 336 1A and 445 in the Twentieth ward; Enumeration District 1058 3B and 1085 5A in the Thirty-second ward; Enumeration District 11 9A in the Thirty-third ward; and Enumeration District 448 in the Fortieth ward. Each enumeration district covers approximately eight to twelve square city blocks.

Chapter 4

[1] For the occupational analysis in this chapter Philadelphia City Directories were used. They were: *Boyd's Philadelphia City Directory* (1910, 1919–1920, 1930); *Polk's Philadelphia City Directory* (1935–1936). Utilizing the author of this book's fluency in the language, Spanish -surnames were located by undertaking a page by page review of these four city directories.

[2] Selected surnames *Boyd's Philadelphia City Directory* (1910 and 1919–1920).

[3] New York, State Census, 1925 for Saturnino Dones, A.D. 15, E.D. 52, p. 34.

[4] U.S., World War I Draft Registration Cards, 1917-1918 for Saturnino Dones. Dones was listed as being "white"; medium height, blue eyes and brown hair. He was 36 yearsold at the time, September 18, 1918. Local Board 24, 1428 Dauphin Street in North Philadelphia.

[5] Pennsylvania, World War I Veterans Service and Compensation Files, 1917-1919, 1934-1948. Veterans Compensation Application # 261572 for Jose DeCelis Serial # 2537833 accessed through Ancestry.com/Military records on 22 July 2016.

[6] Population, corresponding Enumeration Districts for Spring Garden (see Chapter 3 for specific Enumeration Districts).

[7] The sample of Spanish surname was compiled by reviewing the directory for the most common Spanish surnames known to the author.

[8] This interview was part of the Puerto Ricans in Philadelphia class I taught at Temple University.

[9] These patterns were also prevalent among New York City Puerto Ricans in this time period Chenault (1938: 87–8).

[10] *Soup Tureen* (Campbell Soup publication), September and October, 1943 also address labor shortages and the need for workers for the tomato season.

Chapter 5

[1] In writing about Puerto Rican settlement process in the United States in the 1940s and 1950s, Hernández Álvarez developed a model, which isolated the distinct characteristics of a typical Puerto Rican community. Although Hernández Álvarez' model was based on his study of Puerto Ricans of the mid-nineteenth century, it is useful for the earlier decades as well. In Philadelphia, the general premises of Hernández Álvarez' model: geographic location and distribution of Puerto Ricans; the physical characteristics of Latino neighborhoods as evidenced by the growth of professional, commercial, and the types of leadership; the persistence of the Spanish language, customs, and habits for the maintenance of a shared identity as Puerto Ricans; and common interests and attitudes towards assimilation as expressed in popular culture (Hernández Álvarez 1968: 51–2).

[2] The term "Great Migration" and the years 1945–1965 depicting this period is based on general agreement among several scholars (Rodriguez 1986; Center for Puerto Rican Studies 1979) among others argue that in the period between the end of the Second World War and 1965, approximately 1,000,000 Puerto Ricans moved to the United States. It is the largest airborne migration of the modern era.

[3] See also New York's *La Prensa*, 8 May 1929: 6.

[4] By 1920, the 900 block of Marshall Street had become the major business area serving the greater Northern Liberties community. The area was home to many Russian and Polish Jewish immigrants who replaced the German Jews (Krasnow Ellison and Mark Jaffe 1994: 14).

[5] Specifically the records from 1 January 1917 to 1 January 1918. See also "Officers of the Club Juventud Hispana [Hispanic Youth Club]," October 25, 1939, NSC; Spanish Catholic Club.

[6] Both letters (Moreno 1945; Senior 1946) are found at Temple University Urban Archive, Spanish Historical Developments, 1940–1957 (selected years).

[7] For a detail examination of the role of the International Institute/Nationalities Services Center among Puerto Ricans in Philadelphia in the post-World War II period see Whalen (1994: chapter 6).

[8] Gloria Santiago is Lucrecia Cardenas' niece. The letter is the possession of author. See also the 1948 flyer "Dia de las Madres," of the Misión Evangélica (at the Spanish in Philadelphia, NSC, Temple University Urban Archives).

[9] The five-year period, 1941-1946, accounted for 47 percent of the total Puerto Rican migration to the United States in the 38-year period beginning in fiscal year 1908-1909. More than 50,000 Puerto Ricans moved permanently to the U.S. in this period (Senior 1947: 7).

[10] See also *La Prensa*, throughout the 1950s and 1960s.

[11] Koss (1965: 65) found that 65 Puerto Ricans who came to work at the Campbell Soup Company in 1944 were still employed there in 1961.

Chapter 6

[1] For fuller understanding of Puerto Rican state-sponsored labor migration see: Centro de Estudios Puertorriqueños (1979). For specific cases of these programs on certain cities and

regions, see Whalen (2001) and Fernandez (2012: chapter 1).

[2] For other references regarding labor migration and the dispersal of Puerto Rican laborers after WW II, see Whalen and Vázquez-Hernández (2005).

[3] For an understanding of the changing economic picture in Philadelphia after WW II and how the shift impacted African Americans and Latinos in particular, see Goode and (1994), and Adams et al. (1991).

[4] In fact, according to Gonzalez (1987–88), there were probably few other cities in the country, North or South, as racially segregated as Philadelphia.

[5] The fighting originated in a fight between a white and Puerto Rican patron in a bar on Mount Vernon. As a result of that clash, whites began attacking Puerto Rican in Spring Garden, including breaking into a home where they believed the Puerto Rican who was involved in the original fight lived. The invaders proceeded to beat up the residents of the apartment. Large-scale fighting broke along several blocks in Spring Garden. The clashes lasted for almost two weeks. While seven were residents were eventually arrested, only two were charged with possessing knives and none received jail time (Whalen 2001: 184–9).

[6] Wells later wrote *The Modernization of Puerto Rico: A Political Study of Changing Values and Institutions* (1969), considered a classic among several books written about Puerto Rico's economic and political transformation during the late 1940s and 1950s under the leadership of Governor Luis Munoz Marin. In *The Modernization of Puerto Rico*, Wells articulated a discourse of progress and way to redefine a new strategy of territorial governance supported by political platform provided by the Popular Democratic Party (PPD—in Spanish).

[7] This episode led to street demonstrations and a raucous community meeting at the Council of Spanish Speaking Organizations, with city officials demanding justice for the victim. In another meeting with Philadelphia Police Commissioner Joseph F. O'Neill to order a thorough investigation into Osorio's drowning, one of the witnesses, Gilberto Ortiz, said Osorio drowned after being chased by a group of white youths.

[8] In this case the victim was shot to death by a police officer, and the community was pressing the mayor and police departments to fire the officer.

[9] For a full discussion of the presence of the Young Lords Party in Philadelphia, see Whalen (1998: 107–23).

WORKS CITED

Adams, Carolyn T., David Bartelt, David Elesh, Ira Goldstein, Nancy Kleniewski, and William Yancey. 1991. *Philadelphia: Neighborhoods, Division, and Conflict In A Post-Industrial City*. Philadelphia: Temple University Press.

Alfaro, Humberto. 1983. Iglesia de Dios en Vineland: un analisis de su crecimiento integral. Philadelphia: Eastern Baptist Theological Seminary.

Aponte, Edwin D., David Bartelt, Luis A. Cortes, Jr. and John C. Raines. 1994. *The Work of Latino Ministry: Hispanic Protestant Churches in Philadelphia*. Philadelphia: Pew Charitable Trusts.

Archdiocese of Philadelphia. 1910–45. Annual Reports of the Church of the Miraculous Medal—Religious and Financial Statistics for the years 1910-1945. St. Charles Seminary Archives.

Banner-Haley, Charles. 1992. *To Do Good and to Do Well: Middle-Class Blacks and the Depression, Philadelphia, 1929–1940*. New York: Garland Publishing.

Bausman, James. 1987.*Public Housing, Race and Renewal*. Philadelphia: Temple University Press.

Bermudez, Jesse (Jesus Malpica). 1999. Interviews by author. 6 February, 13 May.

Blumin, Stuart M. 1976. Residential Mobility Within the Nineteenth-Centuty City. In *The Peoples of Philadelphia: A History of Ethnic Groups and Lower-Class Life, 1790–1940*, eds. Allen F. Davis and Mark H. Haller. 37–54. Philadelphia: Temple University Press.

Boyd's Philadelphia City Directory. 1910, 1919–1920, 1930.

Business Week. 1944a. 22 April: 10.

———. 1944b. 29 April: 114

Camp, J. Harry and John T. Gillespie. 1975. 20 Demonstrate for Justice in Firebombing. *Philadelphia Evening Bulletin* 8 October.

Canales, Juan. 1999. Interviews by author. 20 February, 1 March.

Carr, Norma. 1989. The Puerto Ricans in Hawaii: 1900–1958. Ph.D. dissertation, University of Hawaii.

Casulleras, Antonio, C.M. 1910. First Annual Report of the Spanish-American Colony. St. Charles Seminary Archives, La Milagrosa files.

Centro de Estudios Puertorriqueños. History Task Force. 1979. *Labor Migration Under Capitalism: The Puerto Rican Experience*. New York: Monthly Review Press.

———. 982. *Sources for the Study of the Puerto Rican Migration, 1879–1930*. New York: Centro de Estudios Puertorriqueños, C.U.N.Y.

Chenault, Lawrence R. 1938. *The Puerto Rican Migrant in New York City*. New York: Columbia University Press.

Cigar Makers History in Philadelphia, PA. n.d. Accessed 28 March 2016. <http://conradkahler2.omeka.net/exhibits/show/https---conradkahler2-omeka-ne/post-war-life/cigar-makers-history-in-philad>.

City of Philadelphia. Human Relations Commission. 1964. Philadelphia's Puerto Rican Population with Census Data.

Colón-Colón, Héctor L. 1983. Iglesia Metodista 'La Resurrección': estudio de una congregación con crecimiento buscando servir a una comunidad en transición. Philadelphia: Eastern Baptist Theological Seminary.

Connelly, James F. 1976. *The History of the Archdiocese of Philadelphia*. Philadelphia: Archdiocese of Philadelphia.

Cooper, Patricia. 1987. *Once A Cigar Maker: Men, Women and Work Culture in American Cigar Factories*. Urbana: University of Illinois Press.

Cutler, William W., III and Howard Gillette, Jr., eds. 1980. *The Divided City: Social and Spatial Dimensions of Philadelphia, 1800–1975*. Philadelphia: Temple University Press.

Davis, Allen F. and Mark H. Haller, eds. 1976. *The Peoples of Philadelphia: A History of Ethnic Groups and Lower-Class Life, 1790–1940*. Philadelphia: Temple University Press.

Delgado, Linda C. 1998. Rufa Concepción Fernández: The Role of Gender in the Migration Process. In *Puerto Rican Women's History: New Perspectives*, eds. Felix V. Matos Rodriguez and Linda C. Delgado. 171–80. Armonk, NY: M.E. Sharpe.

Delgado Pasapera, German. 1984. *Puerto Rico: sus luchas emancipadoras, 1850–1898*. Río Piedras, PR: Editorial Cultural.

Dolan, Jay P. and Jaime R. Vidal. 1994. *Puerto Rican and Cuban Catholics in the U.S., 1900–1965*. Notre Dame, IN: University of Notre Dame Press.

Doucoudray Holstein, H.L.V. 1829. *Memoirs of Simón Bolívar, President Liberator of the Republic of Colombia and of his Principal Generals; secret history of the revolution and the events which preceded it from 1807 to the present time*. Boston: S. G. Goodrich.

Ericksen, Eugene P. et al., eds. 1985. *The State of Puerto Rican Philadelphia*. Philadelphia: Institute for Public Policy, Temple University.

Farr, Gail E. 1994. Register of the Records of the Council of Spanish Speaking Organizations of Philadelphia, 1966–1990. The Historical Society of Pennsylvania.

Fereshetian, Q. 1951. Spanish Community. Temple University Urban Archives, NSC, Folder #13.

Fernandez, Lilia. 2012. *Brown in the Windy City: Mexicans and Puerto Ricans in Postwar Chicago*. Chicago: The University of Chicago Press.

Flores, Juan. 1984. Translator's Preface. In *Memoirs of Bernardo Vega: A Contribution to the History of the Puerto Rican Community in New York*. By Bernardo Vega, ed. César Andreu Iglesias. ix–xii. New York: Monthly Review Press.

Franklin, Vincent P. 1979. *The Education of Black Philadelphia: the Social and Educational History of a Minority Community, 1900–1950*. Philadelphia: University of Pennsylvania Press.

Fretz, Franklin Kline. 1911. The Furnished Room Problem in Philadelphia. Ph.D. dissertation, University of Pennsylvania.

Gillespie, John T. 1975. Children's Fights Let to Hostilities Then Firebomb. *Philadelphia Evening Bulletin* 9 October.

Giusti. Juan. 1975. Progress Report On: The origins of the Puerto Rican community In Philadelphia 1944–1953. Unpublished manuscript.

Glasser, Ruth. 1994–95. *En Casa en Connecticut*: Towards a historiography of Puerto Ricans outside of New York. *CENTRO: Journal of the Center for Puerto Rican Studies* 7(1): 50–9.

———. 1995. *My Music, My Flag: Puerto Rican Musicians and Their New York Communities, 1917–1940*. Berkeley: University of California Press.

———. 1997. *Aquí Me Quedo: Puerto Ricans in Connecticut / Los Puertorriqueños en Connecticut*. Hartford: Connecticut Humanities Council.

Glazer, Nathan and Daniel P. Moynihan. 1970 [1963]. *Beyond the Melting Pot: The Negroes, Puerto Ricans, Jews, Italians and Irish of New York City*. Second edition.

Golab, Caroline. 1977. *Immigrant Destinations*. Philadelphia: Temple University Press.

Gonzalez, Juan D. 1987–88. The turbulent progress of Puerto Ricans in Philadelphia. *CENTRO: Journal of the Center for Puerto Rican Studies* 2(2): 34–41.

Goode, Judith and Jo Anne Schneider. 1994. *Reshaping Ethnic and Racial Relations in Philadelphia: Immigrants in a Divided City*. Philadelphia: Temple University Press.

Greenbaum, Susan D. 1993. Economic cooperation among urban industrial workers: Rationality and community in an Afro-Cuban mutual aid society, 1904–1927. *Social Science History* 17(2): 173–93.

Gregg, Robert. 1993. *Sparks from the anvil of Oppression: Philadelphia's African Methodists and Southern Migrants, 1890–1940*. Philadelphia: Temple
University Press.

Gunter, David. 1975. Puerto Ricans March for Rights, Agree on Bomb Bail. *Philadelphia Evening Bulletin* 30 October.

Haller, Mark H. 1976. Recurring Themes. In *The Peoples of Philadelphia: A History of Ethnic Groups and Lower-Class Life, 1790–1940*, eds. Allen F. Davis and Mark H. Haller. 277–90. Philadelphia: Temple University Press.

Handlin, Oscar. 1959. *The Newcomers: Negroes and Puerto Ricans in a Changing Metropolis*. Cambridge, MA: Harvard University Press.

Hardy, Charles A. 1989. Race and Opportunity: Black Philadelphia during the Great Migration, 1916–1930. Ph.D. dissertation, Temple University.

Hanchett, Thomas W. 2000. Financing suburbia: Prudential Insurance and the post-World War II transformation of the American *city*. *Journal of Urban History* 26(3): 312–28.

Hernandez, Jose. n.d. Telephone interview by author.

Hernández Álvarez. José. 1968. The movement and settlement of Puerto Rican migrants within the United States, 1950–1960. *International Migration Review* 2(2): 40–52.

Hershberg, Theodore. 1976. Free Blacks in Antebellum Philadelphia. In *The Peoples of Philadelphia: A History of Ethnic Groups and Lower-Class Life, 1790–1940*, eds. Allen F. Davis and Mark H. Haller. 111–34. Philadelphia: Temple University Press.

Hershberg, Theodore, Alan Burstein, Eugene Erickson, Stephanie Greenberg, and William Yancey. 1981. A Tale of Three Cities: Blacks, Immigrants, and Opportunity in Philadelphia, 1850–1880, 1930, 1970. In *Philadelphia: Work, Space, Family and Group Experience in the Nineteenth Century*, ed. Theodore Hershberg. New York: Oxford University Press.

Hirsch, Arnold R. 2000. Containment on the home front: Race and Federal Housing Policy from the New Deal to the Cold War. *Journal of Urban History* 26(2): 158–89.

Jackson, Kenneth T. 1987. *Crabgrass Frontier: The Suburbanization of the United States*. New York: Oxford University Press.

Klein, Philip S. and Ari Hoogenboom. 1980. *A History of Pennsylvania*, 2nd ed. University Park: The Pennsylvania State University Press.

Koss, Joan D. 1965. Puerto Ricans in Philadelphia, Migration and Accommodation. Ph.D. dissertation, University of Pennsylvania.

Krasnow Ellison, Elaine and Elaine Mark Jaffe. 1994. *Voices From Marshall Street: Jewish Life in a Philadelphia Neighborhood, 1920–1960*. Philadelphia: Camino Books.

Kusmer, Kenneth L. 1976. *A Ghetto Takes Shape: Black Cleveland, 1870–1930*. Urbana: University of Illinois Press.

La Prensa. 1941. 6 June: 8.

Lewis, Claude. 1975. Fire-bombing of young Puerto Ricans. *Philadelphia Evening Bulletin* 12 October.

Lewis, Oscar. 1965. *La Vida: A Puerto Rican Family In The Culture Of Poverty: San Juan and New York*. New York: Random House.

Licht, Walter. 1992. *Getting Work: Philadelphia, 1840–1950*. Cambridge, MA: Harvard University Press.

McCadden, Joseph and Helen McCadden. 1969. *Father Varela: Torch Bearer from Cuba*. New York: United States Catholic Historical Society, Monograph Series XXVII.

McCaffrey, Joseph D. and Arthur T. Ridgway. 1975. 250 Puerto Ricans March At Scene of Fire-bombing. *Philadelphia Evening Bulletin* 7 October.

Martinez, Fermina. 1923. Letter to Olive Steede, International Institute. 23 February. Nationalities Services Center Collection, Accession # 625, Box #63, Folder #11-Correspondence 1923–1925. Temple University Urban Archives.

Martínez, Manuel. 1989. *Chicago: historia de nuestra comunidad puertorriqueña*. Chicago: n.p.

Massey, Douglas S. 1990. American apartheid: Segregation and the making of the underclass. *American Journal of Sociology* 96(2): 329–57.

Massey, Douglas S., Joaquin Arango, Graeme Hugo, Ali Kouaouci, Adella Pellegrino and J. Edward Taylor. 1998. *Worlds in Motion: Understanding International Migration at the End of the Millennium*. Oxford: Clarendon Press.

Meléndez, Edgardo. 1995. *Puerto Rico en Patria*. Río Piedras, PR: Editorial Edil.

Meléndez, Edwin and Carlos Vargas-Ramos, eds. 2014. *Puerto Ricans at the Dawn of the Millennium*. New York: Center for Puerto Rican Studies.

Metauten, Raymond. 1959. *Puerto Ricans in Philadelphia*. Philadelphia: Commission on Human Relations.

Miller, Fredric M., Morris J. Vogel, and Allen F. Davis. 1983. *Still Philadelphia: A Photographic Essay, 1890–1940*. Philadelphia: Temple University Press.

Mills, C. Wright, Clarence O. Senior and Rose Kohn Goldsen. 1950. *The Puerto Rican Journey: New York's Newest Migrant*. New York: Harper & Brother Publishers.

Mohl, Raymond A. 1982. Cultural pluralism in immigrant education: The International Institutes of Boston, Philadelphia and San Francisco, 1920–1940. *Journal of American Ethnic History* Spring 1(2): 35–58.

———. 1988. The transformation of urban America since the Second World War. *Amerikastudien/American Studies* 33(1): 53–71.

Montgomery, David. 1987. *The Fall of the House of Labor: The Workplace, the State, and American Labor Activism, 1865–1925*. New York: Cambridge University Press.

Morales Carrión, Arturo. 1984. *Puerto Rico: a Political and Cultural History*. New York: W.W. Norton & Company.

Moreno, Isabel. 1945. Letter to Marion Lantz. 8 March.

Mormino, Gary R. and George E. Pozzetta. 1987. *The Immigrant World of Ybor City: Italians and Their Latin Neighbors in Tampa, 1885–1985.* Urbana: University of Illinois Press.

———. 1993. The reader lights the candle: Cuban and Florida cigar workers' oral tradition. *Labor's Heritage* Spring: 4–26.

Morton, Eleanor. 1936. How the International Institute Operates to Bring About a Feeling of Friendliness Among the City's Many Foreign-Born Groups. *Philadelphia Inquirer* 15 July.

The New Catholic Encyclopedia. 2002. Farmington Hills, MI: Gale Publishing.

New York Times. 1918. Men will be brought to U.S. to help on rys, and farms. 20 January.

O'Brien, John C. 1957. Philadelphia Now Third Haven as Puerto Ricans' Haven. *Philadelphia Inquirer* 2 May.

Olmo, Julio. 2013. Telephone interview by author. 5 September.

Ortiz, Altagracia. 1996. 'En la aguja y el pedal eché la hiel': Puerto Rican Women in the Garment Industry of New York City, 1920–1980. In *Puerto Rican Women and Work: Bridges in Transnational Labor.* 55–81. Philadelphia: Temple University Press.

Ortiz, Angel L. 2007. Telephone interview by author. 16 May.

Pajil (Rodríguez), Emma. 1999. Interview by author. 7 March.

Patria. 1892.

———. 1898. 18 January.

Paul, Ruth Frances. 1940. Negro Women In Industry: A Study of the Negro Industrial Woman in the Clothing, Cigar, and Laundry Industries of Philadelphia. Master's in Education thesis, Temple University.

Pérez, Louis A., Jr. 1990. *Cuba and the United States, Ties of Singular Intimacy.* Athens: University of Georgia Press

———. 1993. *Cuba Between Reform and Revolution.* New York: Oxford University Press.

Perez, Martin. 1998 [1985]. Living History, Vineland New Jersey. In *Extended Roots: From Hawaii to New York/Migracion Puertorriquena a los Estados Unidos.* Centro de Estudios Puertorriqueños. New York: City University of New York.

Perillan, Lucia. 1990. The Wise Woman on Second Street—An Oral History of Tomasita Romero: Commentary on life and change for Puerto Ricans living in Philadelphia. Swarthmore College, Pennsylvania. 13 December.

Philadelphia City Directory. 1910–1936.

Philadelphia Evening Bulletin. 1953. Hurt in Fight of 300 at 15th and Mt. Vernon. 18 July: 3.

———. 1954. TITLE OF ARTICLE? 17 April.

———. 1961. Spanish Frank Keeps Tabs on the 15th Ward Puerto Ricans. 4 September.

———. 1971. 40 Puerto Ricans Picket at Temple. 22 November.

———. 1973. 2 Bombs Hit School Closed in Puerto Rican Boy's Drowning. 20 June.

Philadelphia Human Relations Commission. 1991. Report to the Mayor W. Wilson Goode on Public Hearings Regarding Concerns of Philadelphia's Latino Community.

Philadelphia Inquirer. 1953. 7 Hurt as 1000 Clash in Riot. 18 July: 5.

Philadelphia Sunday Bulletin. 1958. Groups Help Puerto Ricans to Life in Philadelphia Area. 16 March.

Ramos, Bem. 2013. Telephone interview by author. 1 September.

Rickle, William. 1996. Interethnic Relations In Hispanic Parishes in the Archdiocese of Philadelphia. Ph.D. dissertation, Temple University.

Rodriguez Mary. 1999. Interview by author. 7 March.

Rodriguez, Pedro. Telephone interview by author. 12 December.

Rodríguez-Morazzani, Roberto. 1994–95. Linking a fractured past: The world of the Puerto Rican old left. *CENTRO: Journal of the Center for Puerto Rican Studies* 7(1): 20–30.

Rome, Adam W. 1994. Building on the land: Toward an environmental history of residential development in American cities and suburbs, 1870–1990. *Journal of Urban History* 20(3) 407–34.

Sánchez-Korrol, Virginia E. 1994. *From Community to Colonia: The History of Puerto Ricans in New York City*. Berkeley: University of California Press.

Santiago, Gloria. 1999. Letter to Mrs. Hilda de la Rosa. 12 December.

Santiago, Rosa. 1994. Interview by author. 10, 13 April.

Senior, Clarence O. 1946. Letter to Marion Lantz. 26 November.

———. 1947. *Puerto Rican Emigration*. Río Piedras: University of Puerto Rico.

Serrano, Wanda. 1994. Carmen Aponte: An Active and Humanitarian Woman in the Puerto Rican Community. Oral history interview. 22 April.

Schneider, Dorothee. 1994. *Trade Unions and Community: The German Working Class in New York City, 1870–1900*. Urbana: University of Illinois Press.

Scranton, Philip. 1989. *Figured Tapestry: Production, markets and power in Philadelphia textiles, 1885–1941*. New York: Cambridge University Press.

Siegel, Arthur, Harold Orlan and Loyal Greer. 1975 [1954]. *Puerto Ricans in Philadelphia: A Study of Their Demographic Characteristics, Problems and Attitudes*. New York: Arno Press.

Sutherland, John F. 1976. Housing the Poor in the City of Homes: Philadelphia at the Turn of the Century. In *The Peoples of Philadelphia: A History of Ethnic Groups and Lower-Class Life, 1790–1940*, eds. Allen F. Davis and Mark H. Haller. 175–202. Philadelphia: Temple University Press.

The Sunday Bulletin. 1977. Jose Reyes' Death Spotlights Troubled Puerto Rican Area: Jobless Rate May Top 44%. 10 July: 11.

Thomas, Lorrin. 2010. *Puerto Rican Citizen: History and Political Identity in Twentieth-Century New York City*. Chicago: University of Chicago Press.

Tirado, Amilcar. n.d. Workers responding to a changing society: The Case of Puerto Rican Cigar Makers, 1898–1919. Manuscript.

Tincom, Margaret B. 1982. Depression and War, 1929–1946. In *Philadelphia: A 300-Year History*, eds. Russell E. Weigley et al. 601–48. New York: W.W. Norton & Company.

U.S. Department of Commerce, Bureau of Census. 1910. Thirteenth Census of the United States: 1910 – Population, Enumerator District No. 931, Sheet No. 7 A.

———. 1920. Fourteenth Census of the United States. Washington, DC.

———. 1930. Fifteenth Census of the United States. Washington, DC.

———. 2010. Twenty-Third Census: 2010. Population Puerto Ricans in the U.S. Washington, DC.

Varbero, Richard A. 1974. Urbanization and Acculturation: Philadelphia's South Italians, 1918-1932. Ph.D. dissertation, Temple University.

Varela y Morales, Felix. 1997. *El Habanero: papel politico, científico y literario*. Miami: Ediciones Universal.

Vega, Bernardo. 1977. *Memorias of Bernardo Vega: contribución a la historia de la comunidad puertorriqueña de Nueva York*. Edited by César Andreu Iglesias. Río Piedras, PR: Ediciones Huracán.

———. 1984. *Memoirs of Bernardo Vega: A Contribution To The History Of The Puerto Rican Community In New York*. Edited by César Andreu Iglesias. Translated by Juan Flores. New York: Monthly Review Press.

Warner, Bass. 1987. *The Private City: Philadelphia in the Three Periods of Growth,* 2nd Edition. Philadelphia: The University of Pennsylvania Press.

Wells, Henry. 1958. The Puerto Rican Community in Philadelphia. A Report for Mayor Richardson Dilworth with Recommendations.

———. 1969. *The Modernization of Puerto Rico: A Political Study of Changing Values and Institutions*. Cambridge, MA: Harvard University Press.

———. 2000. Interview by author. 3 August.

Whalen, Carmen T. 1994. Puerto Rican Migration to Philadelphia, Pennsylvania, 1945-1970: A Historical Perspective on a Migrant Group. Ph.D. dissertation, Rutgers, The State University of New Jersey.

———. 1998. Bridging Homeland Politics and Barrio Politics: The Young Lords in Philadelphia. In *The Puerto Rican Movement: Voices from the Diaspora,* eds. Andres Torres and Jose E. Velazquez. 107-23. Philadelphia: Temple University Press.

———. 2000. Displaced Labor Migrants or the 'Underclass': African-Americans and Puerto Ricans in Philadelphia's Economy. In *The Collaborative City*, J.J. Betancurt and D.C. Gills. 115-36. New York: Garland Publishing.

———. 2001. *From Puerto Rico to Philadelphia: Puerto Rican Workers and Postwar Economies*. Philadelphia: Temple University Press.

Whalen, Carmen Teresa and Víctor Vázquez-Hernández, eds. 2005. *The Puerto Rican Diaspora: Historical Perspectives*. Philadelphia: Temple university Press.

Whiteman, Maxwell. 1976. Philadelphia's Jewish Neighborhoods. In *The Peoples of Philadelphia: A History of Ethnic Groups and Lower-Class Life, 1790-1940*, eds. Allen F. Davis and Mark H. Haller. 231-54. Philadelphia: Temple University Press.

Willging, Eugene P. and Herta Hatzfeld. 1968. *Catholic Series of the Nineteenth Century in the United States: A Descriptive Bibliography and Union List,* second series: part fourteen. Washington DC: The Catholic University of America Press.

INDEX

Made in the USA
Middletown, DE
04 September 2018